Business Process Reengineering — Plain and Simple

Planning to
Successfully Achieve
Dramatic Increases
in Productivity and Profits

Ben Pitman, Ph.D.

Published by

HRD Press

22 Amherst Road
Amherst, MA 01002
800-822-2801
(Fax) 413-253-3490

ISBN 0-87425-308-X

Editorial services by Lisa Wood

Typesetting by Stephen Oringdulph

Cover design by Marcelino Sellas

ABOUT THIS BOOK

The chief aim of this book is to provide you with valuable ideas and insights that will help you achieve dramatic gains in productivity and profits! I hope you find the skills useful. This book provides an overview of business process reengineering so that you will be able to plan your efforts.

You will learn how to:

- Prepare for Reengineering

- Create a Reengineering Vision

- Identify Target Processes

- Design the New Processes

- Understand the Current Processes

- Implement the Design

This one book won't give you all the answers to your questions, but it will give you the foundation to make an informed decision as to whether reengineering is right for your organization at this time. You will *not* emerge an expert, but you will learn enough to start creating a reengineering plan for your organization. You will also learn of many resources you can use to help you along the way.

You *will* be challenged to stretch your mind. I trust that when you put down this book you will be excited about new opportunities for you and your organization.

WHO SHOULD READ THIS BOOK?

This book was written to help *all* levels of people involved in reengineering. When I reviewed the material currently available on the market, I found many conflicting presentations of the principles. Some books were very general and talked primarily to senior executives. Others talked to those who were actually doing the reengineering, and they talked in *very great detail,* so much so that it could easily be overwhelming to all but the experienced reengineer. So I wrote this book, not to be the "Complete Handbook of Reengineering" but rather to boil it down to something that would be useful and yet, at the same time, easily understood by all levels of people who are unfamiliar with reengineering:

- **Top executives.** You may have heard about reengineering, but you are not exactly sure just what it is. You want to know more so you can decide whether or not it is for your organization, but you don't want to spend hours and hours reading thick, detailed books. You need a thorough, concise explanation. This book gives you just that.

- **Executives and managers advocating reengineering for their organization.** You need more in-depth knowledge and empathy of the process so you can adequately explain what it is, what it can do for your organization, and how to support the people who will have to do it. This book gives you just that.

- **Cross-functional teams who will actually manage the reengineering project.** While you may have the inclination to read the more comprehensive texts, you need a straightforward overview to get started and a methodology so you can plan and manage your project. This book gives you just that.

- **Supervisors and front-line workers.** You may be confused and anxious about just what reengineering is and how it will affect you. This book will tell you about the process, even if it cannot tell you exactly what changes will be made in your organization. However, you need to know the process to get a good idea of what is happening and to help you ask the right questions to get the answers you need. This book gives you just that.

HOW TO USE THIS BOOK

This book can be of help in several ways.

- **Individual study.** Because the book is self-contained, all you need is an hour or so for the first reading. If you take an extra hour or two and use a pencil, you can gain even more by completing the exercises.

- **Workshops and seminars.** This book is ideal for use as the text or workbook in a seminar or workshop. An instructor's guide is available from the author, Ben Pitman, 629 Lakeshore Drive, Berkeley Lake, GA 30136-3037, (770) 441-3232.

- **Remote location training.** Copies can be distributed to those not able to attend the training sessions.

- **Informal study groups.** Due to the plain and simple format and the low cost, this book is ideal for informal discussion groups led in-house, by professional associations, or by trained facilitators.

Getting the most from this book

1. Read over the Table of Contents.

2. Flip through the entire book. See what's here.

3. Look over all the appendixes.

4. Go back and read the book slowly, working the exercises.

ABOUT THE AUTHOR

Ben Pitman, Ph.D.

For the past 6 years, Ben Pitman has been helping organizations improve productivity by designing, developing, and facilitating organizational change. Today he specializes in building high performance teams. He bases his advice on experience and a solid theoretical foundation gained while he earned a Ph.D. in Human Resource Development from Georgia State University. In a recent engagement he assisted CSA, Inc., in achieving a 20 percent increase in gross revenue in just three months.

For over 20 years before founding his current company, he managed and developed many information system projects for the State of Georgia, Inforex, Sperry Univac, Consultec, Inc., HAL Systems, Inc., and others. In addition to his computer software experience, his bachelor's degree in Industrial Engineering from Georgia Tech and industrial engineering experience at Lockheed enable him to help manufacturing and engineering organizations.

He has helped numerous companies increase productivity with training courses in systems analysis, project management, time management, communication, motivation, and leadership that he developed and taught.

He is a published author on leadership, motivation, communication, teamwork, and learning with articles appearing in newsletters and a national journal. He has spoken on these topics for the American Society of Training and Development, Atlanta Midrange Computer Users Group, Association for Systems Management, and others.

He is President of the Atlanta Chapter for the Association for Systems Management, a member of the Institute of Management Consultants, the Organization Change Alliance, the Business & Technology Alliance, and the Southeastern Software Association.

Ben is available to answer your questions and help you improve performance anytime. Call him in Atlanta at (770) 441-3232. If he's not in, leave a message and your level of urgency. He returns most calls personally, especially the urgent ones, within 24 hours.

CONTENTS

About This Book   iii
Who Should Read This Book?   v
How To Use This Book   vii
About the Author   ix

INTRODUCTION
UNDERSTANDING BUSINESS PROCESS REENGINEERING   **1**
Why Reengineer?   3
Reengineering Successes   4
What Is Business Process Reengineering (BPR)?   6
Themes in BPR   8
Do You Need Reengineering?   9
Overall Framework for Reengineering   10
Summary   11

CHAPTER 1
HOW TO PREPARE FOR REENGINEERING   **13**
Success Factors   15
Develop Reengineering Teams   16
First Steps for the Executive Management Team   18
Change Management Team Activities   25
First Steps for the Cross-Functional Team   26
Case Study   36
Summary   38

CHAPTER 2
HOW TO CREATE A REENGINEERING VISION   **39**
Preparing To Create a Vision   41
The Eight Steps To Formulating a Shared Vision   42
Acid Test   45
Case Study Continued   46
Summary   47

CHAPTER 3
HOW TO IDENTIFY TARGET PROCESSES   **49**
Focusing Your Efforts   51
Steps To Identify Target Processes   52
Estimate and Create Feasibility Report   53
Case Study Continued   56
Summary   57

CHAPTER 4
HOW TO DESIGN THE NEW PROCESSES   **59**
   Breakaway Thinking   61
   Two Steps To Creating a New Process Design   62
   Creating the High-Level Process Design   63
   Selecting the Recommended High-Level Process Design 65
   Design Reviews   66
   Creating and Selecting the Detail Process Design   66
   Enablers of BPR   67
   Case Study Continued   72
   Summary   74

CHAPTER 5
UNDERSTANDING THE CURRENT PROCESSES   **75**
   Why Map the Current Processes   77
   Mapping the Current — Nothing New   78
   Update Feasibility Report   79
   Case Study Continued   80
   Summary   81

CHAPTER 6
HOW TO IMPLEMENT THE NEW PROCESSES   **83**
   Implementation Planning Questions   85
   Implementation Checklist   86
   Redesigning the Reward System   87
   How *Not* To Reengineer   89
   Case Study Conclusion   90
   Summary and Review   91
   Wrap Up   92

APPENDIX A: WHERE TO GET MORE INFORMATION   **93**

APPENDIX B: REENGINEERING PLANNING WORKSHEET   **95**

APPENDIX C: REENGINEERING PLANNING TIMETABLE   **105**

APPENDIX D: CASE STUDY SOLUTION   **107**

   What Allied Actually Did

APPENDIX E: ANSWERS TO SUMMARIES   **111**

INTRODUCTION

UNDERSTANDING BUSINESS PROCESS REENGINEERING

UNDERSTANDING BUSINESS PROCESS REENGINEERING
Why Reengineer?

Reengineering Successes

What Is Business Process Reengineering (BPR)?

Themes in BPR

Do You Need Reengineering?

Overall Framework for Reengineering

Summary

WHY REENGINEER?

> Unless you change direction, you are likely to arrive at where you are headed. — *Chinese proverb*

Continuing to make improvements to business processes will define tomorrow's true success stories. How much change is necessary? Should you concentrate on incremental improvements or should you attempt to achieve dramatic improvement through business process reengineering? The answer depends on your competitive position in the markets you serve and in your ability to recognize when the status quo is no longer sufficient. Business reengineering represents a thought process which advocates breaking with the rules of the past and creating new rules which will dramatically enhance your ability to compete profitably. Key consideration should be given to the three main drivers of *dramatic* change, which are to:

- Avoid imminent failure when threats from competitors are overwhelming

- Gain a sustainable competitive advantage

- Create future roadblocks for current competitors and/or new entrants

In short, reengineering is about survival!

The intent of reengineering is to make radical changes to core processes that will result in dramatic improvements in:

- Managing costs

- Improving quality

- Improving service levels

- Improving speed of product or service delivery

Business process reengineering represents a major commitment to improving the delivery of products or services and to managing costs. The major reasons for undertaking this dramatic approach can only be determined by the decision makers in *your* organization. **Their total and unwavering support is a critical factor to the success of a reengineering initiative.**

REENGINEERING SUCCESSES

More and more organizations are seeking dramatic gains in performance through business process reengineering.

> On February 7, 1990, American General Corp. announced the decision to consolidate its home service insurance operations in Nashville, Tennessee. A savings of $40 million was realized, and 1,400 employees in Nashville took on, in addition to their own jobs, the work formerly done by 550 employees in Jacksonville. A series of strategic analyses revealed that the company still had some $30 million of overhead that some of the competition did not have. Although many processes had been automated, business was still being done the way it was when the company was organized at the turn of the century. The reengineering program was unveiled in May 1991. The thrust of such a project should be a fundamental rethinking of basic services and systems by challenging everything, including (1) policies, (2) processes and controls, (3) business methods, (4) organizational structure, and (5) service options. As a result of the reengineering process, productivity gains have occurred in a relatively short period of time. Insurance revenues per employees have increased 70 percent since year-end 1990. (From Tuerff, James R., Reengineering the insurance enterprise, LIMRA's *MarketFacts*, Mar./Apr. 1993, Vol. 12, No. 2, pp. 24-28.)

> At Cigna Corp., CIO Raymond Caron's ambitious attempt to align Cigna Systems with the business goals of its reinsurance business resulted in a 52 percent head count reduction, a 1,200 percent transaction time improvement, and a 42 percent operating cost reduction. Under the new system, team effort has replaced individual performance ratings. This gives stronger employees an impetus to help weaker ones improve. (From Margolis, Nell, Voices of Experience, *Computerworld*, Dec. 28, 1992/Jan. 4, 1993, Vol. 27, No. 1, pp. 16-17.)

Organizations are redesigning their underlying business processes to create simultaneous improvement in cycle times, service, quality, and productivity—frequently by orders of magnitude.

Virtually every organization that has been through a major technical reengineering or downsizing effort says the mission ended up being more expensive than anticipated, usually between 30 and 200 percent more. (*Forbes*, March 29, 1993.)

- Ford took a look at its procurement process that employed over 500 people. Management installed a new system to automate the process and cut the headcount by 20 percent. Not bad by most conventional measures. Then it took a look at Mazda. It found that Mazda, a much smaller company, was doing the same function with five people. Adjusting for size, Ford should have been using fewer than 100!

- Litel Communications redesigned its processes for processing new customer orders, reducing the time it takes from 14 days to one and increasing quality at the same time.

- Allied-Signal/Bendix reengineered its process for producing anti-lock bZrakes. The new product designs required 70 percent fewer parts, cutting costs by 60 percent, cutting production time by 50 percent, and cutting time-to-market by 50 percent over a period of 2 1/2 years.

- The 6th annual CSC Index survey of senior information systems executives found that:

  - Business process reengineering was called "most important" more frequently than any other management issue by the 224 U.S. and Canadian respondents.

  - 72 percent said they had a major formal process improvement underway, and another 13 percent were discussing such an effort.

- Clients of consulting firms are reporting return on investment of from 30 to 100 percent.

- According to The Fifth Annual Survey of North American Chief Information Officers in various industries, the average organization more than doubled its number of reengineering projects in 1992.

- A growing number of organizations are reengineering customer service and productivity to realize gains as high as 60 percent.

- To compete in a world market, American organizations are being forced to deliver more solutions, at lower costs, with greater flexibility.

- One organization has learned after 20 years of experience at trying to get better that 50 percent of the cost-savings are in product and process design, 30 percent are in simplifying inventory flow, and 20 percent are in automation.

- A major semiconductor producer reduced its time for delivery from more than a month to two days. This has enabled them to dramatically increase their market share over the past two years.

WHAT IS BUSINESS PROCESS REENGINEERING (BPR)?

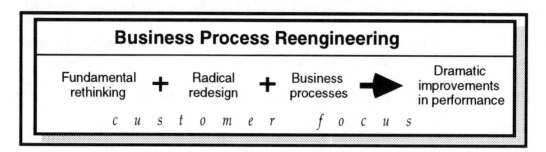

Michael Hammer defines reengineering as **"the *fundamental* rethinking and *radical* redesign of business *processes* to achieve *dramatic* improvements in critical contemporary measures of performance, such as cost, quality, service, and speed."***

- *Fundamental* because it addresses "Why are we doing these things?" rather than accepting the status quo.

- *Radical* because it gets at the root of what is happening, and in most cases discarding what is already in place and starting with a clean sheet of paper.

- *Processes* because it focuses on the core processes, not functions or product lines, that deliver value to the customer.

- And *Dramatic* improvements because it is looking for gains of 50 percent, 100 percent, 500 percent, not 10 percent or 20 percent. If 10 percent or 20 percent is all you need, then look to Total Quality Management (TQM) or Continuous Improvement (CI [or Continuous Process Improvement - CPI]).

Reengineering is a customer focused, top-down effort to establish real breakthroughs in performance. It starts with the attitude that you may well have to completely reinvent how the organization does business. Its purpose is to create new, different, and effective operations, not automate or simply improve existing ones. It is based on customer research, competitive and economic analyses, and benchmarking.

Reengineering goes further than work simplification. First it aims for more radical change at a higher level. Second, it questions the value of a process rather than simply trying to eliminate steps or tasks. Then, and only then, it considers incorporating information technology.

A key principle in BPR is innovation. What is innovation? While the dictionary defines innovation as simply the introduction of something new, we will qualify it to mean something new that gives visible, dramatic results. Innovation is the heart of reengineering.

---

*Hammer, Michael and James Champy, *Reengineering the Corporation: A Manifesto for Business Revolution*, Harper Business, 1993.

While technology is most often credited with the innovation in today's organizations, it is rarely effective without simultaneous innovations in the way we think about the work we do. People have to accept the technology before it can benefit us.

The graph below shows the relationship between Business Process Reengineering (BPR) and Total Quality Management (TQM) or Continuous Improvement (CI). Both are necessary to the growth of a business. Reengineering efforts usually last a short time and have a disruptive impact on a business. After a reengineering effort, the business must stabilize. It may be a long time before another reengineering effort is needed. That's where TQM and CI come in, to smooth out the rough edges.

BPR and TQM/CI

Organization
Performance

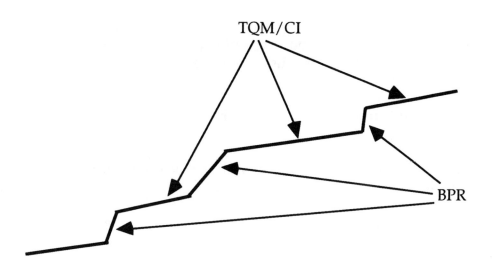

Time

To make a distinction, TQM and CI both ask "How can we perform existing functions better?" They work within the current framework trying to improve processes. Reengineering asks "Why are we doing them at all?" or "How can we eliminate them altogether?"

THEMES IN BPR

- People fundamentally rethink the way work gets done.

- A new value system emerges whereby results are rewarded rather than activity, and advancement is based on ability rather than performance.

- Technology, particularly information technology, is used in new and creative ways.

- There is a strong *process orientation.*

- To achieve the desired results, rule-breaking becomes common.

- Workers make more decisions.

An analysis of current reengineering efforts has revealed these common themes. Some others are listed below. While you may not experience them all, you certainly may look for one or more as you go through your reengineering effort. The point is to prepare for what is to come.

- There is a structural reorganization, usually moving from functional departments to process teams.

- Several jobs are combined into one; people perform multidimensional work instead of simple tasks.

- A new information and measurement system usually comes into play.

- Managers move from bosses to coaches.

- The sponsors have a strong desire to achieve challenging goals.

- A case manager provides a single point of contact.

- Checks and controls are reduced.

- Work is performed where it makes most sense.

A Caution

Reengineering should not be an excuse to reduce staff and teminate employees. If that's all that is happening, it is not reengineering. You have not redesigned your business. All you have done is bought yourself some time. Your competitors will catch and overtake you in short order. You have only delayed the end for a little while.

DO YOU NEED REENGINEERING?

> When it is not necessary to change, it is necessary not to change.
> — *Lucius Cary, Viscount Falkland*

- More than 2/3 of the reengineering efforts fail. [*]
- Reengineering requires a significant investment in extensive in-depth reengineering training and preparation.
- Reengineering requires spending major sums on acquiring the guidance of consultants and experts.
- Reengineering may cause a substantial, gut-wrenching, critically needed shift in your organization's culture.

Reengineering is a risky business.

Reengineering is *not* for everyone. It may *not* be for you. If one or more of the following apply to your organization, you may be in need of reengineering. If not, consider long and hard before beginning a reengineering effort.

❏ Do you need new product development to stay competitive? Are your competitors getting their new products to the market months or years sooner than you are?

❏ Compared to the best in your business, are you employing many more people than you should?

❏ Are your competitors offering similar products at significantly lower prices over a long period of time? (Ignore price wars.)

❏ Are your customers *demanding* significantly faster delivery, better quality, or lower prices?

❏ Is your organization's market share shrinking while the market segment is remaining constant or growing?

❏ Have you tried the other methods of improving your situation (TQM, CI, automation, downsizing, productivity programs) without gratifying results?

❏ Are outside forces (government regulations, economic conditions, technology, etc.) threatening your survival?

❏ Are you getting ready for a major change such as internal reorganization, new computer system, or major automation initiative?

❏ Do you have the data to answer the above questions? (If not, get it before starting.)

[*] Caldwell, Bruce, "Missteps, Miscues," *Information Week*, 1994, No. 480, pp. 50-60.

OVERALL FRAMEWORK FOR REENGINEERING

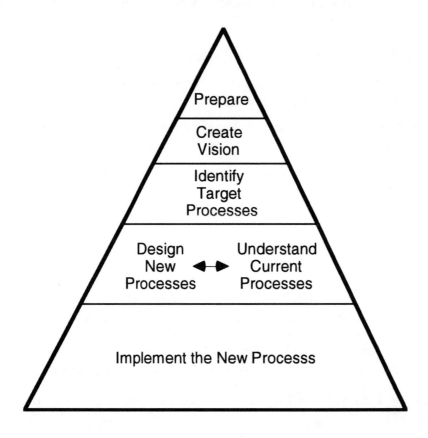

There is nothing magical about the overall framework for implementing reengineering. It is much like that for designing a computer system, adding a new product, or even a major project. Here are the six major steps or phases that have been found to be common to most reengineering efforts. Each is discussed in one of the following chapters. Does one of them seem to be out of sequence?

I.   Prepare for Reengineering

II.   Create a Reengineering Vision

III. Identify Target Processes

IV.   Design the New Processes

V.   Understand the Current Processes

VI.   Implement the New Processes

SUMMARY

Business Process Reengineering is becoming one of the keys to keeping America's businesses competitive in today's global market. Organizations have fundamentally rethought their business processes and radically redesigned them to achieve dramatic gains in performance. Some organizations that have embarked on a reengineering effort have had success. Others have not. This workbook discusses the keys to their success. Don't become a fallout statistic.

• Start by being able to answer the "Do you need reengineering?" questions.

• Get the facts to answer the questions, don't guess.

• Then study this book to learn from those who have accomplished their reengineering goals and from those who missed the mark.

• Apply the lessons learned by writing them below.

The key points I want to apply from this introduction are:

CHAPTER 1

HOW TO PREPARE FOR REENGINEERING

(or Getting Your Ducks in a Row)

I.   PREPARE FOR REENGINEERING
     Success Factors
     Develop Reengineering Teams
     First Steps for the Executive Management Team
     Change Management Team Activities
     First Steps for the Cross-Functional Team
     Case Study
     Summary

SUCCESS FACTORS

1. The MOST CRITICAL factor is a CLEAR BUSINESS NEED FOR THE CHANGE (a clear vision).

2. Second, top management must show clear commitment and leadership for the reengineering effort.

3. There must be proper management of organizational change by avoiding resistance.

4. Operational managers must take an active role and be involved on the teams.

Other success factors include:

- Allocating adequate resources
- Behavioral and interpersonal skills having more importance than technical knowledge and expertise
- Cross-functional teams that are well trained
- No "automation" of the problem
- In-depth knowledge of customer needs and wants
- Integrating information systems and human resource programs
- Identifying, involving, and rewarding process owners
- Managing all the stakeholders through effective communication and inclusion
- Objective outside help such as consultants
- Systems thinking
- Taking a strategic view (customers, competitors, changing business world)
- Comprehensive pilot program
- Follow-through—implementing the redesigned processes

Most successful organizations have developed clear messages about why reengineering is necessary. They support the message with evidence, make it crystal clear and dramatic, and repeat it many times. Consider the nature of ads on TV. Do they send their message only once? Information should be included about the business context, the business problem, why it can't be resolved, and the costs of inaction.

DEVELOP REENGINEERING TEAMS

There are three kinds of teams that usually exist in a reengineering effort:

- Executive Management Teams–select and direct the other teams, sponsor them, and make sure they have all the necessary resources.

- Cross-Functional Process Innovation Teams – are the agents of change. They do all the analysis and design work and guide the implementation.

- Change Management Teams – make sure that the "people issues" in the reengineering effort are properly addressed. If this is left to the cross-functional team, it will not get the attention it needs. The best design is useless if people don't support it.

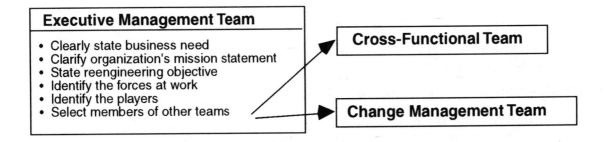

Successful teams always have:

    1. a shared purpose

    2. specific performance goals

Having a meaningful purpose focuses members' aspirations on a common pursuit. Having specific performance goals helps a team set priorities, focus its research, track its progress, and hold itself accountable.

Characteristics of Successful Change Teams

Characteristics for successful change teams include the following:

1. *All stakeholders* are represented.

2. They are a workable size.
   - Can everyone meet easily?
   - Do the members *communicate* well?
   - Is there enough time for all members to participate?

3. They have *complementary* skills, including knowledge of the function, problem-solving skills, and interpersonal skills. At least one member of the information services group should be on the cross-functional team.

4. They have a *clearly defined meaningful goal*.

5. They have decided on *an approach* for working together.

6. *They do what they say* they will do.

7. They are some of the organization's best and brightest!

Other key characteristics include:

8. Interpersonal skills are more important than technical knowledge and expertise.

9. Change teams can spend at least 50 percent of their time on reengineering. This includes the executive team. (A study by McKinsey & Organization revealed that without this commitment the efforts came up far short of projections and with this commitment they were mostly on target.)

Sponsoring executives must ensure that the teams are constructed properly and incorporate the characteristics listed above. Failure to do so will jeopardize the project and maybe even the viability of the business.

FIRST STEPS FOR THE EXECUTIVE MANAGEMENT TEAM

- Clearly state your critical business need
- Clarify key elements of your organization
- State your reengineering objective
- Identify the forces at work
- Identify the players
- Select members of other teams
- Schedule team training

The executive management team gets the ball rolling. They develop the initial focus and ensure that there is a solid foundation on which to build the reengineering program.

Clearly State Your Critical Business Need

All too quickly, people jump to action. Sometimes they have a clear picture of the need, but in the majority of cases the business need is not clearly stated. Frequently there is disagreement about just what it is. This step avoids much later confusion and gives focus to all following activities. It ensures that the first critical success factor is met.

Ask yourself what business need is so critical that you must tear down a good portion of what you are as an existing business and rebuild it.

Key Organizational Elements

These elements need to be communicated to the reengineering teams. The elements provide a clear picture of the context for reengineering and the questions teams can ask themselves.

- Customer definition .... Who are our customers and what are their needs?

- Products/services definition .... What are our primary products or services? What business should we be in?

- Market information .... What threats and opportunities are present in the marketplace now and in the foreseeable future?

- Organization's purpose .... What is the primary purpose of our organization? (This is sometimes called the prime mission. It should be short, 25-50 words, and in a language that everyone from the top to the bottom can relate to.)

- Vision .... What is our corporate vision? The vision statement describes what the world would be like if our organization was living its purpose perfectly.

- Strategy and structure .... What strategies are we using to achieve our vision? How will we be organized?

The Executive Management Team clarifies these key elements of the organization. These elements are frequently the result of high-level strategic planning. If they haven't been clarified, **reengineering is premature.**

State Your Reengineering Objective

The next step for the Executive Management Team is to state in one or two sentences what you are trying to accomplish with your reengineering effort. This normally ties directly to the business need stated earlier. Frequently it is simply a restatement of that business need in terms of something to be accomplished by the organization. It should state what improvements in critical contemporary measures of performance, such as cost, quality, service, and speed, are needed.

Identify the Forces at Work

Before you begin to make radical changes in your organization, you should have some understanding of the forces at work. List the forces **for** and **against** you (and the rest of your organization) in your effort to reach your objective. To indicate the size of the force that may be acting on the reengineering effort, draw large arrows for strong forces and small arrows for weaker forces. We have given you the most likely force in each direction to get you started. You will want to add to this list as you go on.

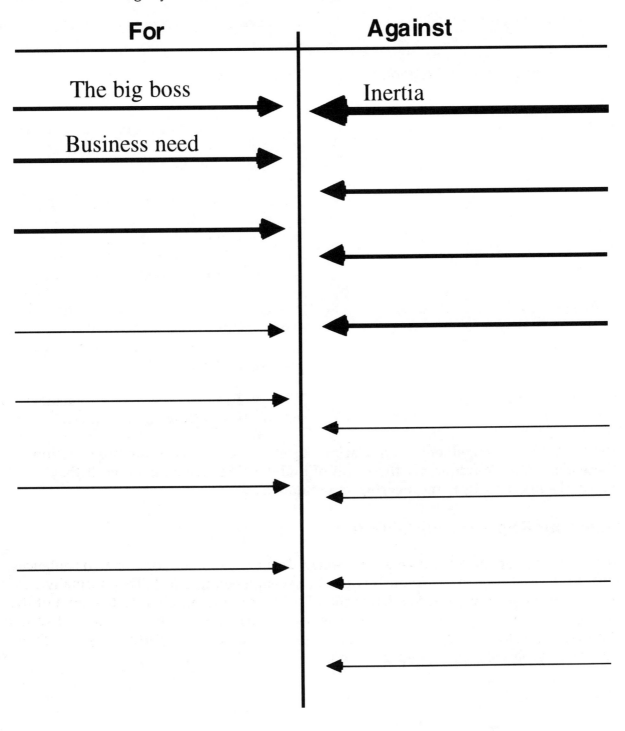

Identify the Players

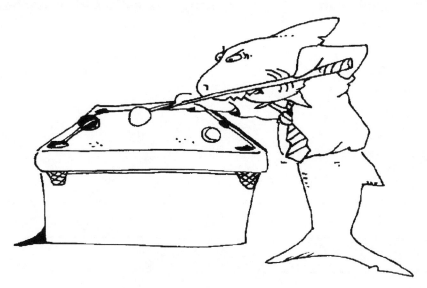

Another way to clarify the forces at work is to identify who will be involved in the reengineering—the players. Daryl Conner, President of Organization Development Resources, has identified four sets of players in the organizational change game.

1. The change **advocate** is the one who proposes change but lacks sponsorship (implementation power).

2. The change **sponsor** is the one who legitimizes the change and has the power to make it happen.

3. The change **target** is the group of people who end up being directly affected by the change.

4. The change **agent** is the group who implements the change.

These players are not always different people. In fact, it is advisable to have many of the change targets be change agents to get commitment to the new process.

Here is a domestic example:

Your mother/father in-law decides that your kids need to take skating lessons. That in-law convinces your spouse that your kids need to take skating lessons. You get to see to it that your kids take skating lessons (what a surprise). Who is the

Advocate? _____

Sponsor? _____

Target? _____

Agent? _____

Next, try this on your own organization. Describe a change taking place (or that has taken place) in your organization.

Identify the

Advocate? _____

Sponsor?   _____

Target?   _____

Agent?   _____

Select Members of Other Teams

By this time the Executive Management Team has a clear picture of what is to be accomplished, the forces at work, and who the players are. Together these will give the team an idea of the chances of success. The next step is to identify who will be on the Cross-Functional Process Innovation Team and the Change Management Team. These teams must have the discretion to add other members as they see fit.

Who will be on the cross-functional team?

- Dedicated project director (manager) _____

- Facilitator _____

- Information technology specialist _____

- Financial/budgetary specialist _____

- Business area specialist (expert) _____

- Affected business unit representatives _____

  _____

  _____

  _____

The Executive Team must make sure that high-quality people are selected for these teams. They must also pick them from a wide range of people, from top to bottom in the organization. Doing so will help ensure that each group is represented in the redesign and each group has an opportunity from the very beginning to contribute to the effort. Failure to do so is to invite massive resistance down the road when the changes are being implemented.

Who will be on the change management team?

Schedule Team Training

The components for training include:

- Reengineering (you can use this book for starters)

- Organizational change[*]

- Systems thinking

- Modeling (statistical modeling as well as software packages)

- Interviewing (knowing how to ask questions to get the data you want)

- Teamwork (sometimes called team building). Teams need to clarify the elements in the Team Layer and develop skills to be effective and get the best results.

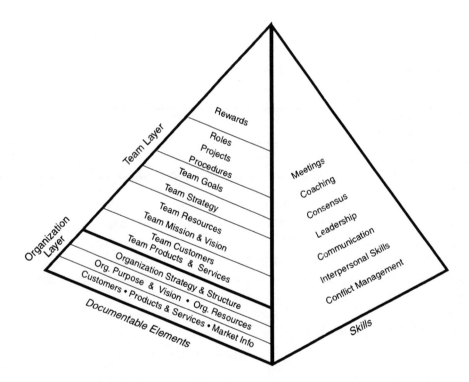

Teams need training to be more effective. Throwing people together in a room and saying "Your job is to" leads to a lot of confusion and low productivity. Training and coaching in how to be a high performance team will dramatically increase the results. Training for the executive team will be generally at a higher level and focused on understanding rather than doing.

[*] See Scott, Cynthia D. and Dennis T. Jaffe, *Managing Organizational Change*, Crisp Publications, Los Altos, CA, 1989.

CHANGE MANAGEMENT TEAM ACTIVITIES

The change management team has the prime responsibility for addressing culture changes in the corporation. The biggest obstacle you will encounter is people's resistance to change.* Some of the activities the team might engage in are:

- Managing expectations

- Ensuring that the reasons for the changes and all changes are communicated

- Ensuring that people are involved in designing the changes that will affect them

- Developing transition structures

- Helping people understand the stages of change (denial, resistance, exploration, commitment)

- Coaching the other teams in how to deal with resistance

Other activities include:

- Updating business policies

- Changing work methods and decision-making methods

- Facilitating the restructuring of the organization

- Designing and implementing new job positions

- Clarifying performance objectives and measurement systems

- Facilitating the redesign of reward systems

---

* Caldwell, Bruce, "Missteps, Miscues," *Information Week*, 1994, No. 480, pp. 50-60.

FIRST STEPS FOR THE CROSS-FUNCTIONAL TEAM

Getting organized for change means thinking about where you want to go, where you are now, and how you are going to get there. Other than the first, there is no particular order in which you should take these steps. Give each some consideration.

- Review and clarify the business need, objective, and forces
- Decide on consultants
- Adopt systems thinking
- Select a process modeling language

Review and Clarify the Business Need, Objective, and Forces

The cross-functional team is a team of people who will design and implement the reengineering project. Its members begin by reviewing and clarifying the mission, the objective, and the forces in play identified by the executive management team. This will give them the context in which they are operating. The cross-functional team may suggest additions or changes to the business need, objective, and forces.

Decide on Consultants

The next step for the cross-functional team is to decide which, if any, consultants they are going to use. Consultants can be a deciding factor in the success of a reengineering effort. They can come from inside or outside your organization. The illustration below shows six reasonably self-explanatory roles consultants can take on during the process.

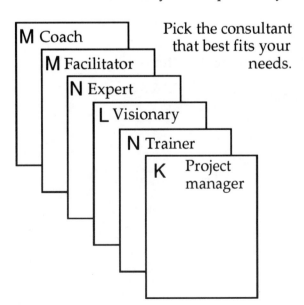

Pick the consultant that best fits your needs.

Note that they are not sponsors or targets. They may be change advocates. They may be part of any of the teams (agents). They do NOT make up the entirety of the change agents. That is to say, people from outside the organization rarely, if ever, can come into an organization and successfully, permanently change it.

Adopt Systems Thinking

Systems thinking is the framework, a way of thinking holistically about things. It requires that you see the forest *and* the trees.

There are seven things to think about:

1. Inputs or Inflows – what's coming into the system from outside.

2. Structure – how things are organized.

3. Processes – what's going on, how things are happening

4. Content – what's being processed (products, customers, patients)

5. Outputs or outflows – what's coming out of the system

6. Outcomes – the impact of the outputs on the rest of the world

7. Feedback – information from the world on how you are doing. It is a special and very critical kind of input.

Sometimes there is some confusion about the differences among structure, processes, and content. Here are two examples that provide clarification.

1. For a organization that delivers the products, the structure is the people, machines, and equipment, and how they are organized. The processes are what the people and machines do. The content is what is being manufactured, the raw materials, and products.

2. For a service business, such as a hospital, the distinctions are less clear. The structure is how the building and machines are laid out and how the people are organized. The processes are the services delivered. The content could be considered to be the medicines and advice dispensed *or* it could be considered to be the patients. What are the raw materials and what transformations are they undergoing?

As you move forward in your reengineering effort, it will be critical that you adopt a systems thinking approach to all you do.

Select a Process Modeling Language

A modeling language should be able to show six of the seven elements in systems thinking. (The element of feedback is excluded.)

1. Inputs or Inflows – what's coming into the system from outside including speeds, frequencies, and volumes.

2. Structure – how things are organized

3. Processes – what's going on, accumulations, flows (information and physical material) between one process and the next as well as delays (queues) along the way.

4. Content – what's being processed

5. Outputs or outflows – what's coming out of the system

6. Feedback

One of the most important steps the cross-functional team will need to take will be to model the new and current processes. The team needs to select a modeling language. The consultants selected may have some ideas about which language is most relevant to their business.

You use the modeling language (set of symbols) to draw a process-flow diagram. This diagram simply shows in graphic form what is going on in the process. The next page shows three sets of symbols used by different disciplines. You may choose to develop your own.

Modeling Language

	Computer Modeling Package	Industrial Engineering	Computer Software Development
Process (Operation)	Batch Process / Conveyor Process	(rounded rectangle)	(rounded rectangle)
		none	none
Inspection	(Considered a process)	(rectangle)	none
Transportation or Flow	Flow / Control Information	→	→
Storage	Storage	(triangle)	(rectangle)
Delay	Queue	(half circle)	
Off-Page Connector	None	(circle)	(circle)
Decision	None	(diamond)	(diamond)

Computer Simulation – Modeling Tools

People are *good* at laying out the *structure* of a system but. . .

- They *aren't so good* at being able to describe the *dynamic behavior* of a system, or where the bottlenecks will be.

Computers *don't do well* at laying out the *structure* but. . .

- They are *GREAT* at exploring the *dynamic behavior* of a system.

Computers help you accurately answer the question, "Would more or less of _____ make a significant difference?"

A process will be limited by its slowest subprocesses. Use the computer model to stretch the limits or capacities to see what the model is sensitive to.

The recommendation is to find and use a modeling tool. Three are described below. Whichever one you choose, be sure to review the Modeling Tool criteria given later in this chapter.

1. Texas Instruments Inc. (TI) recently began shipping its first business processing modeling product. Business Design Facility is a workstation-based system that permits users to graphically model business procedures and organizational structures.

2. NCR Corp. recently unveiled ProcessIt, a group of work-flow process management software that will allow users to design, monitor, and reengineer business processes throughout the enterprise.

3. ithink by High Performance Systems (603) 643-9636) is available for both Windows and Macintosh. Its symbols were shown on the previous page. It satisfies almost all the criteria given later in this chapter. (See Appendix A for complete contact information.) A demo version is available.

These modeling tools can model anything from service production to human resource productivity. Several examples are given on the next several pages for your review. They were all produced using the ithink software by High Performance Systems.

Service Production*

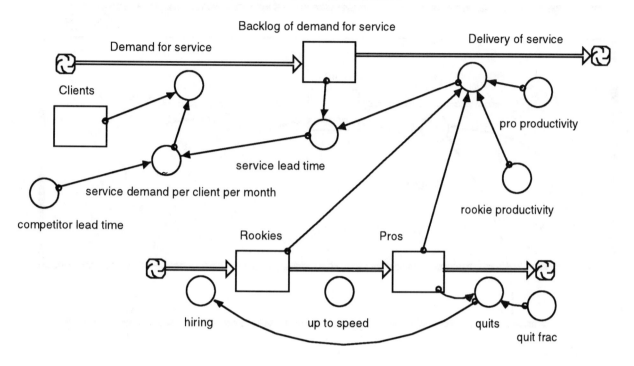

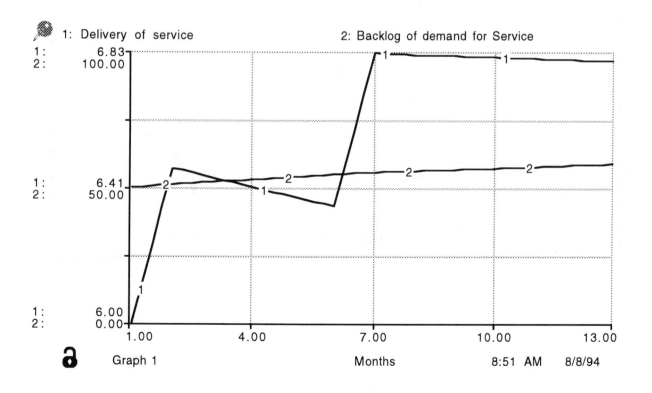

Inventory Labor Management*

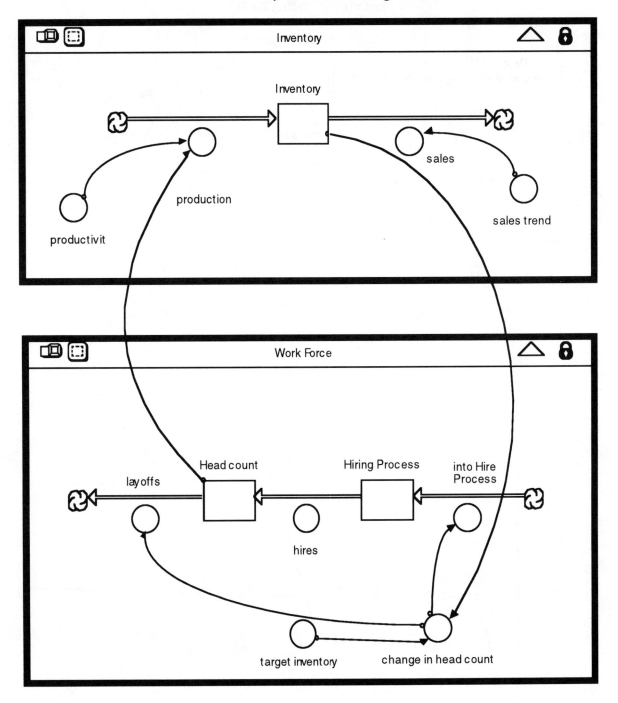

Human Resources Process*

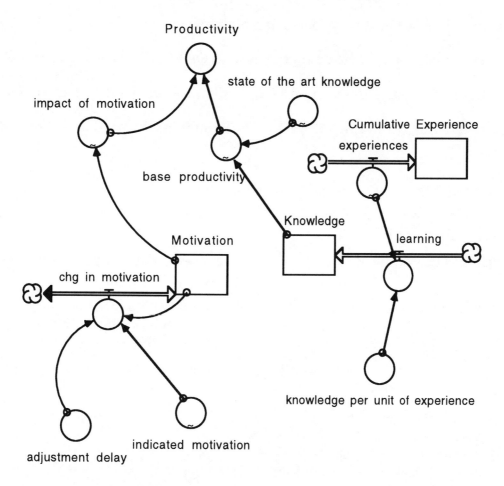

Selecting Modeling Software

The main reason you want to use some type of modeling is to identify where the bottlenecks are.

Thomas Davenport (in his book *Process Innovation: Reengineering work through Information Technology*, Harvard Business School Press, Boston, MA 1993) cites four criteria for selecting a computer-based modeling tool:

1. It should be fast and easy to use at a high level.

2. It should be able to be used on the new as well as the current processes.

3. It should provide a descriptive view of the process as well as an analytical view.

4. It should support multiple layers of detail so it can be used as a design aid.

Add to this list:

5. It should be graphical . . .	because models that depend only on written text are difficult to visualize.
6. It should use a limited number of symbols. . .	so that it can be quickly learned. (One tool available has well over 50 different symbols.)
7. The symbols used should be reasonably intuitive. . .	and easy to relate to the business at hand.
8. It should show what is flowing and the flow rates, what is accumulating and volumes, what is being processed and how long it takes, and delays.	
9. It should show graphs and tables. . .	of what is happening over time as well as tables of the details when conducting simulations.
10. It should enter flow rates, processing times, etc. in graphical form. . .	because it's faster and many times the complex mathematical formulas are not known.
11. It should be able to be used in a variety of "what-if" modes. . .	so you can *easily* vary some of the parameters such as flow rates, capacities, and volumes.

If you decide to use an automated tool, then use the symbols associated with it. If you should decide *not* to use an automated modeling tool, then you will need to develop your own set of symbols.

"People support what they create."

CASE STUDY

(This is a case study of a real organization. The name and several other pieces of information about the organization have been changed to protect the organization's identity and to highlight the reengineering principles discussed in this workbook. This case study focuses on a service aspect of the organization's business because all organizations have at least one service component.)

Allied Manufacturing was continuing to lose its market share. A manufacturing TQM initiative had been started about 5 years ago. Product quality had improved and for a while it looked like the problems were fixed. But then it started to lose more customers. It seemed that customers were buying from competitors who were offering the same products at lower prices.

A quick analysis of the situation by Allied's president revealed that if they did not correct the situation they might have to close some of their plants within 2-4 years. Determined not to let this happen, he called together the board of directors and presented his findings. They agreed that something needed to be done.

Next he called a meeting of the top executives. He again presented his findings along with the recommendations of the board. After some discussion and blaming each other, they agreed with the board's recommendations. The ten executives in attendance selected five of their members to form an Executive Reengineering Team. The team members included the following: VP of manufacturing, VP of marketing, the chief financial officer, director of human resources, and director of purchasing. *(Allied clearly had top management support.)*

The current mission statement of the organization was "to be the number one provider of doctor's office medical supplies in the country." (Note that being number one, while an admirable goal, says nothing about the customers and their needs.)

CASE STUDY EXERCISE: EXECUTIVE TEAM GETS STARTED

You are part of the Executive Management Team. The CEO is a "fad surfer" (riding the crest of the current fad and then paddling out to ride the crest of the next one — witness the programs on excellence, TQM, and continuous improvement in the last 10 years.)

1. As a team do you think Allied needs reengineering? Why?

2. What is your reengineering objective?

3. With the limited information available, what forces do you see at work?

   For   *Against*

4. Who are the players?

5. Who should be on the cross-functional team? (Example: one person from manufacturing, . . .)

SUMMARY

For a reengineering effort to be a success, adequate preparation is necessary, just as it is in any other endeavor in life. This chapter has outlined the major problems you will need to overcome. The biggest one will be inertia, the tendency for the organization to continue as it has in the past. Remember, if you want to keep on getting what you're getting, keep on doing what you're doing!

We looked at the factors that will determine your success. The top three were having a

_____ _____ _____ for the change, having

commitment from the _____ , and properly managing

_____ _____ .

Once you are aware of the factors determining your success, it's time to get organized.

You must: know your _____ , what forces are at work, who the players are,

assemble your teams, determine if you are going to use a consultant and locate one if

necessary, and select your modeling tools.

Training is then in order for the teams. Train in teamwork, in the overall process of reengineering (this book), in organizational change, in systems thinking, and in the modeling tools you plan to use.

The rest of this guide gives the remaining steps or phases in reengineering. The three teams work together to accomplish them. The executive team monitors progress, provides resources, and makes critical decisions. The change management team becomes more involved as the redesigned organization takes shape. It takes a very active role as the transition plans take shape and during implementation.

The key points I want to apply from this chapter are:

CHAPTER 2

HOW TO CREATE A REENGINEERING VISION

Vision: The art of seeing things invisible.
— *Jonathan Swift*

Vision without action is merely a dream.
— *Unknown*

I. PREPARE FOR REENGINEERING

II. CREATE A REENGINEERING VISION
    Preparing To Create a Vision
    The Eight Steps To Formulating a Shared Vision
    Acid Test
    Case Study Continued
    Summary

PREPARING TO CREATE A VISION·

Visions are sometimes confused with dreams. John F. Kennedy had a vision in 1961: "This country will put a man on the moon and return him safely by the end of the decade." There were some who thought this to be a dream. There were many who questioned the President on "How are we going to do that?" A visionary, however, does not have to know "how to," but identifies and gains belief in the "what" and rallies the rest of the folks with the special knowledge to set the right wheels in motion.

Now here we are, celebrating the twenty-fifth anniversary of Neil Armstrong's "One Giant Leap for Mankind" and few of us remember it started with a vision. Visions can be created out of a strong desire to reach supremacy or as a reaction to a significant emotional event. In Kennedy's case, the event was Sputnik and it was a challenge to American technological leadership. Little did President Kennedy know that this vision would set the stage for a technology battle between the East and the West that would lead to the downfall of communism. Visions, once shared and personalized, have the power to change the world in ways never initially considered. An organization, community, or country without a vision today is in a battle for survival in this last decade before the twenty-first century. Visions can be created as a result of strong leadership or a significant emotional event. Which will it be for your organization?

A vision must be specific enough to allow people to internalize and personalize it, but general enough to remove any personal doubts about the possibility of achieving it. There will always be doubters, but there will be many believers who will commit themselves to its success as long as the leadership provides frequent communications and empowers them to participate in the implementation phase.

A vision is not what you will do tomorrow. It should be far enough into the future for everyone to focus on it without being encumbered with the problems facing them today. A vision cannot be a one person view. It must be a shared vision. It should include individuals from outside as well as inside your enterprise. Therefore, consider using customers, suppliers, vendors, directors, as well as employees from all facets of the business.

The visioning process itself can be relatively short in duration. The research and data gathering leading up to the session itself can span several weeks. Also, success is based 15 percent on having the right vision and 85 percent on organizing to implement it in a timely fashion. Visions can certainly be developed internally, but with the rapid changes going on globally and technologically, an outside consultant can bring insights, experiences, and a process to enhance the probability of success greatly. Many times asking the tough questions at the right time requires an outsider's perspective and the visions and strategies created may evolve into a more substantial and sustainable competitive advantage for the enterprise.

· The majority of the material in this chapter was contributed by Brad Lightner, a Senior Partner with Visions Unlimited, Inc. Used with permission. For more information on developing a powerful vision for your company, contact Brad at (404) 410-7627.

THE EIGHT STEPS TO FORMULATING A SHARED VISION

> If you don't know where you're going,
> you'll probably end up somewhere else.

A vision is a description of what you want your ideal future to look like.

The eight steps to take the lead toward formulating a shared vision are:

1. Review your organization's business purpose
2. Understand the "waves of innovation"
3. Exploit the industry's "experience curves"
4. Know your industry's "power relationships"
5. Incorporate your "extended enterprise"
6. Identify your customers' objectives
7. Write a vision statement
8. Check the vision statement

1. Review Your Organization's Business Purpose

You should have a clear definition about what business you are in. Be able to answer in one sentence the question, "Why does this organization exist?" Forget answers related to stockholders, owners, and making money (unless this is a financial business like an investment organization). Instead, focus on what function this organization is supposed to be able to perform. What contribution is it supposed to be making to the planet? Make people happy? Transport goods? Improve productivity? Help people learn about. . . ?

2. Understand the "Waves of Innovation"

Technology by itself is not going to differentiate any organization. However, if it becomes standard practice within an industry to use technology to communicate and share information with customers and you are not capable of exploiting this technology, survival will be questionable at best. Technology that adds value in your relationship with your customers, vendors, suppliers, or consumers can create a differentiating competitive advantage. Tie your success directly to the success of your extended enterprise. This means that selection of your key extended enterprise partners must be successful businesses in their own right and be interested in a win-win relationship.

What are the waves of innovation in your industry? What are the applications of technology which save money? Make money? Grow the pie? What is your competition doing in this area?

3. Exploit the Industry's "Experience Curves"

Determine new ways in which the organization can exploit industry and functional experience curves and compare your experience with competition. Experience curves relate to how the industry is adopting new technologies. When a new technology is introduced, it gives the "early adopters" an advantage. As time goes on, others get on board and adopt the technology, gradually eliminating the competitive advantage. If your vision is to give you a substantial edge over your competition it must answer questions such as:

- What technologies are being introduced that will supersede current methods?
- How are investments being made to change the industry?
- Where is your organization relative to the rest of the industry?
- How can you change the industry to gain a substantial and sustainable competitive advantage?

4. Know Your Industry's "Power Relationships"

Key to knowing where you are going is to know the key linkages within your organization and within your industry. It is important to know which of these linkages are important to your enterprise's survival and what potential changes can occur. An example is the Wal-Mart scenario that eliminated the use of wholesalers between the retail operations and the manufacturers. If you were the wholesaler, how would you continue to do business with Wal-Mart? Likewise, knowing the experience curves that are occurring within your industry and where you are relative to these changes is key to having a competitive advantage vision. If you are a retailer without Point of Sale (POS) devices, and the industry is using POS to track and replenish inventory, are you a viable competitor in this industry?

5. Incorporate Your "Extended Enterprise"

Before any organization can reengineer, it must know the other organizations with which it interacts to conduct business. This extended enterprise has many elements. Some examples of these elements are customers, wholesalers, retailers, suppliers, buyers, consumers, government agencies, and any other external organizations important for an organization's success. In some industries, the extended enterprise can contain as much as 87 percent of the cost of products or services sold by an enterprise. Therefore reengineering your business without understanding the cost impact in the extended enterprise will allow for control of only 13 percent of the pie. What are the key elements of your organization's extended enterprise? What can you do to help your customers be more successful?

6. Identify Your Customers' Objectives

To adequately serve your customers, you need to be very clear about their critical needs and expectations. You need to find out what you can do to make your customer more successful. Do this by talking to the customers, not guessing in the board room.

You want answers to questions such as: "What is your organization's mission? How can we help you sell ____ more profitably? What can we do to make your job easier? What problems do you have? What help do you need?"

There are many tools adaptable from market research you can use. It is risky to rely on just one method. Using two or three will help you "triangulate" the real needs. Here are the most common ones.

- One-on-one interviews with customers. If you deliver services to another business, talk to the heads of the customer organization as well as the people who come in direct contact with your organization. The president may have one view of what is needed while the purchasing agent or the receiving clerk may have an entirely different view.

- Focus groups—getting several representative customers together to discuss how things could work better

- Surveys

- Returns—if you sell a product, examine the reasons for returns

- Complaints—examine what people have been complaining about

- The competition—what features or benefits are they stressing in their promotion

- Reasons for lost sales—find out why your prospects rejected your proposals and accepted someone else's. Why do potential customers buy from someone else?

7. Write a Vision Statement

Describe what your organization will look like if you achieve the reengineering objective. Make it a stretch from where you are, an aggressive target. Think about:

- What will your customers be saying?
- What will they be able to do differently as a result of your changes?
- What will the members of your organization be saying?
- How do you want them to feel?
- What aspects of the physical environment will change? Of your service? Of your product?
- Is it short, sweet, and inspirational?

Here's an example: "Our vision is to be the recognized center of knowledge in the world in the field of mechanical engineering, helping those who need this knowledge to be more successful."

8. Check the Vision Statement

Does it:

- Take advantage of the waves of innovation?

- Use new power relationships?

- Incorporate the industry experience curves?

- Employ an expanded extended enterprise?

- Help customers be more successful in selling their products and services?

- Motivate and inspire?

- Stretch people and move them toward greatness?

- Communicate easily? (clearly? simply? concretely?)

- Seem achievable?

- Fit with corporate values?

ACID TEST

Your vision should give you a substantial and sustainable competitive advantage. Michael Porter, in a 1985 *Harvard Business Review* article entitled "How Information Gives You Competitive Advantage," stated that a substantial competitive advantage must alter industry structures and rules, support cost and differentiation strategies, or spawn entirely new businesses.

Part A: Is your vision substantial? Does it:
1. Alter industry structures and rules?
2. Support cost and differentiation strategies?
3. Spawn entirely new businesses?

Part B: Is your vision sustainable? Do you have the resources to attain and maintain it?

An advantage may be substantial, but if it can't be sustained it offers little hope of meeting the three criteria. Also a small advantage may be sustainable, but if it isn't substantial enough to meet one of the three criteria it becomes relegated to being an incremental change. Insanity has sometimes been defined as doing a little bit more of the same and expecting different results.

CASE STUDY CONTINUED

[Due to the limited time you may have available and the limited knowledge you may have of the industry described in the case study, we will focus on only one of the many aspects of creating a vision described above. The others are equally important.]

Who are our customers?

The cross-functional team began the process of creating a reengineering vision. First they made sure that they were clear just who their customers were. A meeting, facilitated by the consultant, revealed that while doctors' offices were their ultimate customers, regional distributors and dealers were their immediate customers.

Customer Objectives

The team formulated a plan to gather data about the real needs. Marketing offered a recent market research report that would save them much time. The team reviewed the report and decided that it was too broad and did not specifically address their past and current customers.

CASE STUDY EXERCISE: DEVELOP A PLAN TO GATHER DATA

You are now on the cross-functional team. Your current task is to develop a plan to gather data to be sure that you are addressing the correct processes and get firmly connected with the customer's needs.

SUMMARY

Creating the vision is key to determining the direction of the reengineering effort. To attain a substantial and sustainable competitive advantage, you must consider:

- The waves of innovation

- New power relationships

- Industry experience curves

- Expanded extended enterprise

- Customer needs with customer-based data

Then ask yourself, "Does this vision motivate and inspire?" "Does it communicate easily?"

Finally, be sure your vision is substantial (alters industry structures and rules, supports cost and differentiation strategies, or spawns entirely new businesses).

Is your vision sustainable? Do you have the resources to make it happen?

CHAPTER 3

HOW TO IDENTIFY TARGET PROCESSES

What Makes You Valuable to Your Customer

I. **PREPARE FOR REENGINEERING**

II. **CREATE A REENGINEERING VISION**

III. IDENTIFY TARGET PROCESSES
   Focusing Your Efforts
   Steps To Identify Target Processes
   Estimate and Create Feasibility Report
   Case Study Continued
   Summary

FOCUSING YOUR EFFORTS

Before getting into the core of redesign, you need to bring focus to your work. Without focus on the core processes, you may well waste time, and lots of it, on areas that are not important. In this step you are looking for the processes that are the most important to delivering value to your customer.

A process is a specific ordering of work activities across time and place, with a beginning and an end, and clearly identified inputs and outputs. Here are some examples of core business processes.

Process	From	To	Critical Performance Measure*
Customer communication	internal data information	customer quality	time
Customer support	inquiry	solution	response time
Engineering design processes	?	?	?
Management	capital vision	product direction	development time
Manufacturing capability development	bare ground	a factory	construction time
Manufacturing	raw materials	product quality	lead time, cost
Market strategy development	chaos	concept	development time
Marketing	concept	program	
Order fulfillment	order	payment	order cycle time
Product development	concept	prototype	time to market
Research processes	ideas	workable concepts	time, cost, competitive ideas
Sales	prospect	order quality, quantity	sales cycle time,
Logistical or support processes including human resource	?	?	?
Business strategy development			

---

*   Four basic measures form the foundation of almost all Critical Performance Measures. Two measures we continually aim to reduce are *time* and *cost*, and two we aim to increase are *quality* and *quantity*. Most all measures are some combination of these four. For example, profit is sales in dollars (a quantity) less the costs (a quantity); productivity is quantity divided by time and cost.

STEPS TO IDENTIFY TARGET PROCESSES

There is a tendency to focus on "broken processes," ones that obviously need help. Be cautious about spending too much time on these at first, because you may decide to totally eliminate them in the new design. Follow these steps:

1. Start with your organization's mission statement, a statement about what your customers are buying, and your reengineering vision statement. These should already be available from the work you have done previously.

2. Make a first attempt at naming your one main process that implements your mission and delivers what your customers are buying.

3. List associated processes. Brainstorm all the processes that are part of the one main process.

4. Identify the "from" and "to" parts for each process. For example, order fulfillment becomes "Order fulfillment: from order to payment." See the list on the previous page for more examples.

5. Add support and planning processes such as strategy development, marketing, selling, and accounting. Separate the parts of accounting into the external connections that link to the customer and the internal parts that relate only to your organization.

6. Now organize these, linking one to another. *Organize around outcomes*, not tasks, functions, or products. A good starting place, but not the only one, is to begin with the customer and work backward.

7. Identify 4 to 7 core processes, the ones that create the added value that the customer is buying. Try to limit yourself to 4 to 7 processes so that the project is manageable.

    Deciding where to draw the line between one core process and the next can be difficult. One way to make the decision is to imagine a process owner—the one person in the organization who will be ultimately responsible for that entire process. The imaginary process owner would have control over the process from beginning to end. If it makes sense for the process owner to have control over the subprocess, then make it part of the core process. If you can't decide, you can leave it until the redesign because it is not critical. Remember the purpose of this step is to focus your efforts, not make final process design decisions.

8. Identify what's flowing between the core process and the other processes, core and non-core. Put each core process in the center of a sheet of paper. Set the scope of what you are trying to do. Be careful not to overcommit your resources.

9. Finally, determine your performance measurement. Be able to answer the question "What performance results am I trying to improve?" See the examples listed on the previous page in the "Critical Performance Measure" column.

ESTIMATE AND CREATE FEASIBILITY REPORT

Reengineering is not cheap. It is not something you can afford to jump into without some serious consideration and analysis. By this point in the reengineering process you know much more about the situation than you did at the start. It is time to formalize what you have discovered and make a conscious decision whether or not to proceed.

One way to do this is to create a feasibility report. It should summarize what you have learned so far including these elements:

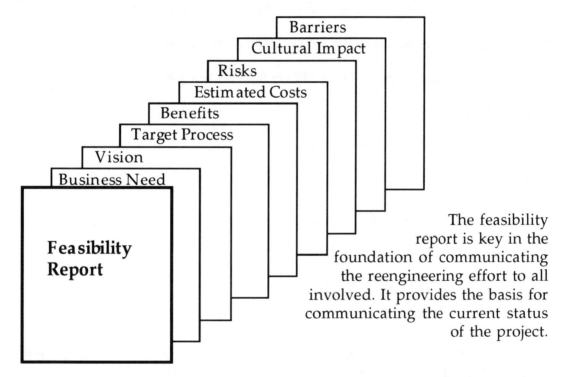

The feasibility report is key in the foundation of communicating the reengineering effort to all involved. It provides the basis for communicating the current status of the project.

- The clear business need for the reengineering initiative. This should include what is likely to happen if you *don't* reengineer.

- Your reengineering vision

- A list of the target processes to be reengineered

- The potential benefits from reengineering in terms of the critical performance measures (cost savings, increased flexibility, reduced cycle time. . .)

- The estimated costs of the reengineering effort in dollars, time, and other resources (see the following page)

- A brief description of the risks involved

- The effects the reengineering effort is likely to have on the organization's social system and culture

- The existing barriers that must be overcome to make the effort a success

Estimating Time and Costs for Reengineering

For the first three phases, Preparation, Visioning, and Identifying Target Processes, respectively, see Appendix C: Planning Timetable for a starting point.

For the fourth phase, Designing the New Processes, and the fifth phase, Understand the Current Processes, guidelines are difficult to provide, because they depend on the size and complexity of the processes involved. Also, reengineering is new and we have very little historical data to work with.

In some ways we are a lot like the explorers Louis and Clark on the first journey across North America. We can only estimate as far as we can see. So you may have to adopt an incremental estimating process and estimate the next phase only.

The time necessary to complete the project will depend on the:

- number of processes you have chosen to reengineer

- complexity of those processes

- amount of change to those processes—the bigger the change, the more time

- shift in technology used—the bigger the jump, the more time

- intensity of the need for change

- strength of the organization's leadership

- amount of resistance from the organization

- size of the organization and the number of business units

- length of time the organization has been functioning as it is today—the longer it has, the harder it will be to get it to shift direction

Following are some thoughts regarding these estimates:

A very rough rule of thumb is that it will take as long to properly design the new processes as it will to analyze and document the current ones (collect data, draw the process-flow diagrams, create a computer model). That is, you will probably spend as much time collecting data about how new technologies work for the new design as you will collecting data about how the current ones work.

Larger, more complex processes will take longer to design than smaller, simpler ones.

Breaking large processes down into smaller ones will make them easier to estimate.

Therefore, to estimate the design phase (IV), estimate the understanding phase (V) by breaking it down into smaller processes and estimating how much time you will spend gathering data and creating the process-flow diagrams.

The biggest step, implementation, is even harder to estimate because it depends entirely on the outcome of design.

You can't let the whole process, including implementation, cost more than it must save.

In most cases, the implementation will take much longer than the rest of the entire reengineering effort and our **best guess** at this point is that it will take about twice as long as phases IV and V together. It will also take 2 to 10 times the effort.

To express this as a formula:

Est. = Prepare + Vision + Target + Design New + Understand Current + Implement

> Design New (unknown) *approximately* = Understand Current (which you know something about)

> Larger processes = {Small + small + small + ...}

> Implement *approximately* = 2 x (Design New + Understand Current)

Michael Hammer, who co-authored *Reengineering the Corporation,* says you should be nearly done in a year. He claims that if you let it take longer than that you will fail because inertia will get in your way and people won't believe that you are really changing things. Given this point, you may decide to limit the scope of what you are trying to reengineer.

Another report indicates that reengineering projects often take a year or more in the formulation phase and 12 to 24 months for the implementation phase.*

Analysis of some efforts have revealed a distribution something like this:

Process	Percentage
Prepare	5
Vision	10
Target Processes	5
Design New	10-15
Analyze Current	5-15
Implement	50 -65

---

* Davis, Tim R. V., "Reengineering in Action," *Planning Review,* July/August 1993, pp. 49-54.

CASE STUDY CONTINUED

Target Processes

In Allied's case it was easy to get started identifying the target process. The hard part was setting a scope—what was to be considered part of the order fulfillment process and what wasn't. The current process began when a sales representative took an order and continued until it left the plant. This order crossed the boundaries of sales, order entry in accounting, credit checking in accounting, and shipping. What was clear was that the people involved in these areas were each doing their job and not really concerned with the other areas.

CASE STUDY EXERCISE: OUTLINE FEASIBILITY REPORT

Your current task is to rough in the feasibility report. Take your best guess as to what it would look like. Make any assumptions you need to make.

SUMMARY

The first step after you are organized is to determine which processes are to be reengineered. This focuses your effort, improving your chances for success.

Begin with your organization's _____ and what your customers are buying from you. Understand clearly their _____ . List all the processes you can think of. Then organize them and try to consolidate them into _____ (how many) main processes. The ones you are looking for are the ones that _____ _____ for the customer.

The key points I want to apply from this chapter are:

CHAPTER 4

HOW TO DESIGN
THE NEW PROCESSES

Looking For New Ways

I.   **PREPARE FOR REENGINEERING**
II. **CREATE A REENGINEERING VISION**
III. **IDENTIFY TARGET PROCESSES**

IV. DESIGN THE NEW PROCESSES
     Breakaway Thinking
     Two Steps To Creating a New Process Design
     Creating the High-Level Process Design
     Selecting the Recommended High-Level Process Design
     Design Reviews
     Creating and Selecting the Detail Process Design
     Enablers of BPR
     Case Study Continued
     Summary

BREAKAWAY THINKING

One of the main differences between reengineering and other forms of process improvement is that **reengineering starts (almost) with a blank sheet of paper.** Reengineering requires leaving the existing process design and starting all over again by asking "If I could start from scratch, what would the perfect process look like?" (NOT "How can I make *this process* better?").

The point is that you must break away from the old ways of doing things. You must break away from the existing rules and assumptions that underlie the current process and break through to new, more productive and effective rules and assumptions. An excellent example of how challenging rules and assumptions can lead to dramatic changes in process design and improvement is at Ford Motor Organization. The now famous scenario was Ford's rule that a payment was made at the time an invoice was received. The new rule became a payment would be made on delivery of the goods. The new rule permitted a complete redesign of Ford's accounts payable process and a 75 percent reduction in head count. An even newer rule being contemplated now is that payment will occur at time of sale of the goods.

New and Current at the Same Time

While the phases of Designing the New Process and Understanding the Current One are presented one after the other in this text, in practice, reengineering teams flip back and forth between the two, now designing the new, then looking back at the current, then back to designing. So, read these two chapters in order, but remember that in practice, you will design some, then examine the current and find aspects or processes that need to be changed in the design.

TWO STEPS TO CREATING A NEW PROCESS DESIGN

Designing a new process is an awesome but an excitingly creative undertaking for any reengineering team. Designing a new process is hard work, but it can also be fun. Above all, redesigning a process should not be intimidating. To minimize the fear and bewilderment a reengineering team might feel as it starts its task of coming up with a new process design that will vastly outperform the current one, a sort of "divide-and-conquer" approach should be used; that is, you break down the design task into two major steps.

Step 1: High-Level Design	**Step 2: Detail Design**
High-level understanding	In-depth understanding
Major process steps/flow	Subprocess/task steps/flow
Key HR/IT levers	Specific requirements
Estimated impact	Cost/benefit analysis

The High-Level Process Design

During the first step, the reengineering team creates what is known as a *high-level process design.* The high-level design is a "big picture" view of how the new process will work and the expected benefits. It is supported by a high-level flowchart depicting the major process steps and how they interact. The high-level design is also called the conceptual design or overall design.

Appropriate time and resources should be given in developing the conceptual design because it is during this time that breakthrough performance enablers and capabilities can be easily explored. Major changes are made at this stage. The farther along you get, the more expensive it will be to introduce new ideas and ways of doing work.

The Detail Process Design

During step two of process design, the reengineering team creates a *detail process design.* The detail design depicts, as precisely as possible, how the process and its subprocess will work. In addition to a detail flowchart (down to task level) of the new process, the detail design also includes specific requirements for:

- *human resources* (e.g., staffing levels, job descriptions, skill requirements)

- *technology* (e.g., hardware, software, outsource partners, equipment)

- *facilities* (e.g., space, furniture, phone)

CREATING THE HIGH-LEVEL PROCESS DESIGN*

Before the reengineering team starts its quest for a high-level process design, it should first revisit the objective(s) of the reengineering initiative. With the objective(s) clear to every member, the reengineering team is ready to begin developing a high-level process design.

One way to approach the "big picture" design is through a series of process design workshops in which the reengineering team meets and brainstorms completely new ways for performing the process. Teams have found the following principles and techniques extremely helpful in creating new, higher performing process designs.

Some Process Redesign Principles and Techniques

- Organize around outcomes not tasks, functions, or products.

- Design processes for simultaneous processing and link steps in real time.

- Extend the process to customers and/or suppliers.

- Benchmark "best-practice" organizations with similar processes.

- Capture all critical information once and at the source.

- Have those who use process output perform the process. Have those who produce the output use it.

- Treat geographically dispersed resources as though they were centralized.

- Use information technology to create completely new process designs.

Key Process Innovation Questions

- Without worrying about any constraints (time, money, technology, etc.) what would the "ideal process" look like?

- What current rules and assumptions can we break to enable dramatic improvement in process performance?

- How can we adapt proven principles of process redesign to enable dramatic improvement in process performance?

- How can we adapt today's information technologies to enable dramatic improvement in process performance?

---

* Thanks to Jim Brewton for his ideas in this section.

- What "best-practices" can we adapt to dramatically improve process performance?

- What's thought impossible today but, if it were possible, would dramatically improve process performance?

Creating the Right Environment for Innovative Thinking

To maximize success, process redesign workshops must be conducted in an atmosphere where creativity and innovative thinking can flourish. The following guidelines can help you create the right environment for your reengineering team:

- Recognize redesign as an art, not a science.

- Use redesign principles and techniques as tools, not rigid methodologies.

- Allow for a full flow of creative ideas, passing no judgment or evaluation during brainstorming process innovation concepts.

- Go for quantity at first. Quality can come later.

- The wilder the idea the better—this can lead to true breakthrough solutions.

- Use idea generation tools (see Appendix A).

- Use the Idea Generation Grid discussed later in this chapter.

A Word of Caution

Reengineering teams can often limit their creative options by focusing on technology as the "only answer" or looking for "best-practices" to speed the creation of new process design approaches. While both are good ways to generate innovative process designs, they should not be used alone. They should be used along with looking for "non-technology" enablers and viewing their process as "unique."

Also remember to use information technology to create completely new process capabilities, *not* to automate the current process.

SELECTING THE RECOMMENDED HIGH-LEVEL PROCESS DESIGN

The reengineering team will finally reach a point when it has exhausted its ideas for new process design concepts.   The time will come to select the best high-level process design from several the team has identified through its process design workshops. The team should settle upon a concept selection methodology that allows the most objective means of evaluating each candidate concept. The following provides one methodology that has been used successfully for this purpose:

High-Level Design Selection Process

- Select at least three, and preferably more, objective criteria for evaluating each concept (*e.g., cycle-time, cost, product quality, service quality, etc.*).

- Weight each criteria based upon its relative importance among all criteria. You can use a scale of 0-5 or 0-10 for low to high importance. You can use negative weights for criteria to make the alternative less attractive. For example, as the risk level goes up, the overall score of the alternative should go down. See the weight (wt.) column below.

- Establish rating standards that measure how each design alternative rates on each criteria (*e.g., 0 Non-existent, 1 extremely low, 2 low, 3 neutral or moderate, 4 high, 5 extremely high*).

- Evaluate each high-level process design by multiplying the rating times (x) the weight of the criteria (see the Score column). Then total the scores.

Once the recommended high-level design has been selected, the cross-functional team should meet with the Executive Management Committee to present its recommendations and to seek approval for continuing the process redesign initiative.

Criteria	Wt.	Alternative 1		Alternative 2	
		Rating	Score	Rating	Score
Cost	5	1	5	2	10
Competitive edge	7	2	14	4	28
Implementation time	3	2	6	3	9
Future flexibility	4	4	16	3	12
Risk level	-3	1	-3	4	-12
Barriers	-2	3	-6	4	-8
TOTAL:			26		39

DESIGN REVIEWS

While the Cross-Functional Team may have done its best to consider all aspects necessary in the redesign, it is not uncommon to have missed something. Some teams have found it very beneficial to have the designs reviewed by front-line supervisors and workers at this point. This keeps them informed and involved in the project and much more likely to support the changes later on. They may even be able to help rate the various alternatives and add criteria that were overlooked.

The Cross-Functional Team may stop at this point to have their selection reviewed by the Executive Management Team. One effective way of doing this is to update the Feasibility Report. By keeping this document updated along the way, the team can begin to get a handle on how the project is changing from its original inception. Knowledge of these trends may be very valuable later on as the project expands.

CREATING AND SELECTING THE DETAIL PROCESS DESIGN

With the high-level process design selected and approval to continue with reengineering the process obtained, the team now must develop the detail process design. Developing a detail design is an iterative process and is enhanced by using the process redesign principles already discussed. The reengineering team first takes each major process step from the high-level design and brainstorms specific ways in which the step can be performed that will enable the achievement of reengineering objectives.

Each step or subprocess should be broken down to the task level. The team should brainstorm, from subprocess to task level, exactly who might do what, when, and how, and with what possible tools. With an exhaustive list of alternatives, the reengineering team must, again, select what they believe is the best process design. A methodology similar to the one used for the high-level design can be used for the detail design selection process.

Upon completion of the detail design, the reengineering team may again have it reviewed by front-line supervisors and workers to get their input and keep them informed. Then they would update the Feasibility Report and present their recommendations to the Executive Management Team.

ENABLERS OF BPR

Human Resource Enablers

Your work as a reengineer will fundamentally change the way your organization operates. Here is a list of typical shifts that organizations have found enabled them to reengineer the human aspect when they moved from functional or product orientation to a process orientation. They are your human resource enablers—areas that enable people to put all that fancy technology into action.

Area	From	To
Work units	Functional departments	Process teams
Job design	Simple tasks	Multidimensional work: wider variety of skills, more steps in the process, seeing the end result
Decision making	At the top	At all levels, subordinates involved
Reward systems	Based on activity	Based on results (See Reward System in Implementation Phase)
Values	Protective; Satisfy the boss	Productive; Satisfy the customer
Managers	Bosses	Coaches
Executives	Scorekeepers	Leaders
Job preparation	Training	Education
Advancement criteria	Performance	Ability
Organizational structures	Hierarchical	Flat
Communication	Mostly downward	Up, down, lateral
Policies	Limiting	Freedom to make many more decisions when needed

During your design, look for these changes. If you do not see them, then consider what reengineering you would have to do to see these shifts. It may give you more ideas on how you can improve the process. For example, if you don't see more decisions being made at lower levels, ask, "What would happen to _____ (critical performance measure) if we let workers make more decisions?"

Team and Organization Elements

The shifts (from-to) shown on the previous page are all part of moving from a traditional hierarchical organization to an empowered team-based one. All team activities are based on organizational needs. If organizational needs aren't clear, then teams will function at less than optimum. To make that shift effectively the elements in the organization layer shown below must be firmly in place.

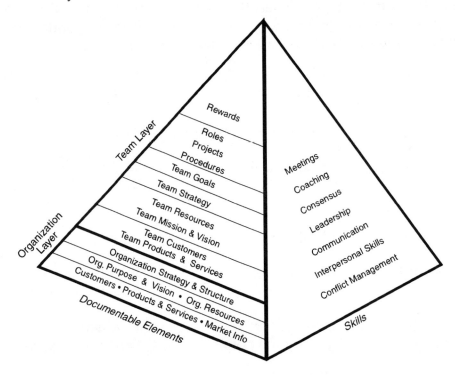

The elements in the team layer are much more likely to change with time than those in the organization layer. People join and leave the organization. Needs change. Teams must be able to regroup and refocus quickly to maintain a competitive organization.

Procedures for Establishing the Team Elements

Teams need to develop a set of procedures that spell out how they will determine elements in the team layer. For example, when departments are reorganized, as they frequently are during reengineering, it usually takes a while to clarify the team goals and the roles of team members. If the organization has a set of documented procedures that it uses to establish these goals and roles, work proceeds much more quickly, with less conflict, and the team is much more productive. They also need the skills shown above.

Information Technology Enablers

- Application Programmer Interfaces
- Client/server Architecture
- CD ROM
- Electronic Data Interchange (EDI)
- Electronic Mail/EM Filters
- Electronic Notebooks
- Expert Systems (artificial intelligence)
- Graphical User Interface (GUI)
- Groupware
- Hi-Performance Workstations
- High Bandwidth Networks
- Image Processing

- Intelligent FAX
- Interactive Videodisk
- ISDN
- LANs/WANs
- Mini/mid-range Computers
- Modeling Tools
- Multimedia
- Neural Networks
- Object Oriented Programming
- OCR
- Optical Disk Storage
- Parallel Processing
- Rule-based Workflow
- Shared Databases
- Smart Cards
- Video Teleconferencing
- Voice Recognition
- Voice Synthesis
- Wireless Communications

Impacts of Information Technology

- Eliminate manual labor

- Improve decision making in ways that would be impossible without high-speed calculations

- Provide information previously unavailable such as tracking and detailed case histories

- Multiple people can work on same document at the same time

- Less skilled people can do the work of higher skilled

- Instantaneously sharing data across great distances

- Power to less skilled or disabled, e.g., voice recognition and pen-based computing, are bringing computing power and capabilities to those who were previously limited

Idea Generation Grid: Using the Enablers To Generate Ideas

An idea generation grid takes a list of enablers and helps you to apply them to areas you might not have considered. It is a very simple process and usually has best results when you use a facilitator to keep things on track. This was originally designed to be used on a spreadsheet (grid), but it became too crowded. A summary spreadsheet may be helpful at times to see if ideas in one area can be used elsewhere.

- Put the name of a process at the top of the page.

- Make list of enablers with space to write between each.

- Brainstorm how each enabler could improve the process.

- Make copies, one set for each process (core, major, or subprocess) you wish to reengineer.

The idea grid makes sure you have considered applying each enabler to each process. (See the example on the next page.)

Order Entry Subprocess

Human Resource Enablers

Skill Variety

CAT teams do order entry plus. . .

Task Identity

*Follow orders from beginning to end
Identify with customers more*

Reward Systems

Reward adopting new system

Technical Enablers

Client/Server Architecture

?

CD ROM

Show client uses of new products

Graphic User Interfaces

Make it easier for sales representatives to learn new system

Expert Systems

*Aid in product selection and credit problems
Suggest alternate products*

Mobile Computers

Sales representatives enter orders in field

Interactive Videodisk

Show client uses of new products

Voice Recognition

Make it easier for sales representatives to enter orders

CASE STUDY CONTINUED

The New Process Design

The cross-functional team incorporated some new information technology for entering the orders. The salespeople would enter the orders directly into notebook computers. The notebook computers would immediately check the order for accuracy. Once the entire order was entered, the salesperson would phone in and connect his/her computer with the central computer and send the orders. While still connected with the central computer, the system would check inventory and customer credit. If all was okay, the order was printed right there at the customer's site. Corrections could be made immediately; problems with inventory availability and credit could get quicker resolution.

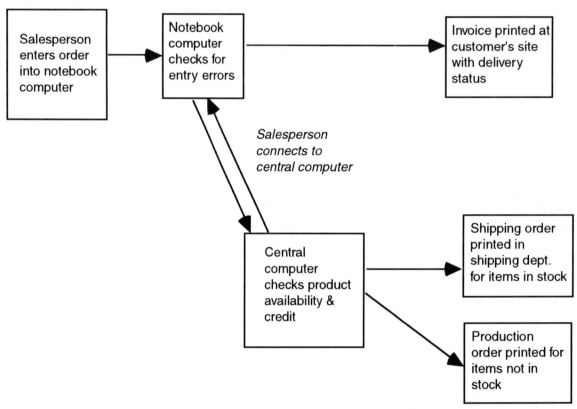

With production orders now connected directly to customers, salespeople can check on production status while connected to the central computer.

They did some benchmarking with two other firms that manufactured products and distributed them to dealers. The team found order receipt to shipping cycle time on nonexpedited orders ranged from 4-10 hours; 9 percent of orders shipped had errors; and cost per order averaged 4 percent of revenues. These numbers would be useful after comparable measures for their own organization were gathered in the next phase.

In addition, the order entry staff and several accounting clerks were combined to form a Customer Assistance Team (CAT). The entire customer list was divided among pairs of people on the team. The team chose pairs instead of individuals so that each person had a backup for lunch, vacations, etc. Each CAT pair supported the sales representatives that covered the customers. The CAT responded to individual requests by sales representatives and direct inquiries by customers. They tracked orders from the time they were entered by sales and made sure that production orders were on schedule. They reviewed any delay notices printed by the computer and expedited the procurement of raw materials if necessary to get the orders back on schedule. The new computer system would track costs related to customers in each CAT, which enabled management to award bonuses to the CATs based on performance.

Some performance measures used were average time to ship, correct order percentage, and quarterly customer satisfaction rating.

Managing Change

The Change Management team got more involved during the design phase. As the new design began to take shape, they arranged two sets of meetings with each affected department. In the first set they gathered ideas about how things could be improved and in the second set they presented the draft of the new process design and asked for further improvements. A set of meetings proved to be a requirement rather than a single one because everyone could not attend a single meeting.

| CASE STUDY EXERCISE: COMPARING CASE STUDY TO THIS GUIDE |

Only an inventor knows how to borrow, and every man is or should be an inventor. — *Ralph Waldo Emerson*

Since redesign requires an in-depth knowledge of the current processes, we will take a slightly different approach in this activity. Your task is to compare the design principles given in this guide to the case study.

What principles and technologies did they use? How?

What other principles or technologies might they have used and how?

SUMMARY

We covered a great deal in this chapter. We learned that BPR is different from other performance improvement techniques in that it _____ _____. The reason? To break away and attain a fundamental rethinking and radical new design of the processes to attain those dramatic improvements.

The two key enablers of reengineering are_____ _____ and _____ _____ By rigorously looking for ways to apply each enabler, you can attain dramatic gains in performance.

The key points I want to apply from this chapter are:

CHAPTER 5

UNDERSTANDING THE CURRENT PROCESSES

I. PREPARE FOR REENGINEERING

II. CREATE A REENGINEERING VISION

III. IDENTIFY TARGET PROCESSES

IV. DESIGN THE NEW PROCESSES

V. UNDERSTAND THE CURRENT PROCESSES
Why Map the Current Processes
Mapping the Current—Nothing New
Update Feasibility Report
Case Study Continued
Summary

WHY MAP THE CURRENT PROCESSES

> Experience is a hard teacher—first it gives the test and the lesson comes afterward.

Once you have identified the target processes AND have some idea where you want to go, you need to get more information on the current state of affairs. It is unlikely that any one person completely understands the entire process. People may ask "Why should we spend all this time mapping out the current processes if we are going to change them anyway?" Here are several answers to that question.

To facilitate communication

Reengineering teams usually bring together people from all parts of the organization. They think differently. They have different languages and points of interest. Mapping out the current processes will force everyone to adopt a common language. Without it you will have difficulty communicating among team members, which, as you remember, is a key to success.

To avoid repeating solved problems

As part of the effort you will identify mistakes of the past and make sure that you won't repeat them. Input from front-line supervisors and workers is critical here.

To measure value

Once you get to the new processes, management will want to be able to measure the improvement. Without a base line of the old system, it will be very difficult to measure the value of the new system.

To help move from the old to the new

Eventually you will have to move from the current way of doing business to the new. Chaos will reign if you just try to impose the new process. You must plan your move from the old way to the new way so that you can continue to do business while the move is taking place. It will do you little good to develop the best processes in the world and lose all your customers in the move.

MAPPING THE CURRENT—NOTHING NEW

Your purpose in this step is to map and measure the existing processes at a level between very high and very detailed. To describe the current processes you need a methodology that will include a description of how to understand and communicate about the current and future organization. This includes a description of the inputs, structure, processes, content, outputs, and outcomes.

You create a business process model that is a representation of an operation or process. It is usually a graphical depiction of the structure and activities of the operation. The model shows the relationships between work steps and their sequence. Together these portray work flow.

It should show all activity and the relationships between each department's mission and the activity the department performs.

Key information includes activity description, volumes, frequencies, how long activities take, resources required, value added by the activity, information required, inputs, outputs.

Work at the document level, not the data element level. Although data elements are important to information engineering, business processes are usually defined in terms of document flow, not data element flow. Managers and executives understand documents and are not usually interested in the details.

You will need to:

• Agree on the elements of the process (system) to be considered and their names. (See Systems Thinking in Chapter 2.)

• Agree on a modeling language, a set of symbols to represent the processes.

The skills and knowledge you develop in this step will be very useful when you prepare for implementation. You will need a new process model at the same, or perhaps even greater, level of detail than when you map the current processes. This is not an easy task. It takes time to develop the mental skills needed to quickly model a process.

Remember:

"All models are wrong, some models are useful" (paraphrasing Deming).

"The best model is as simple as possible. . . but no simpler" (paraphrasing A. Einstein).

UPDATE FEASIBILITY REPORT

Now you have an even better idea of what it will take to reengineer your business. Before continuing, you should update your feasibility study to make sure that your reengineering will pay off.

- You may well want to revise your vision and the target processes to be reengineered.

- You may have found some additional benefits.

- You definitely need to revise your estimates on how much time and how much it will cost to implement the reengineered processes.

- You probably know more about the risks you will face and may have found some additional ones.

- By now your Change Management Team should be involved and they should assess the impact of the reengineering on your organization's social system and culture.

- And finally, you may have a better handle on the barriers that must be overcome.

The Executive Management Team will want to review the project status at this point. It is here that a "go/no-go" decision will be made. Up to now nothing has been changed. The teams have just considered possible changes. Proceeding beyond this point will incur great costs and sometimes great risks to the organization. Executive approval and support is critical at this point.

This updated feasibility report will provide the basis for more communication to everyone in the organization. You don't need to communicate the entire report. The Change Management Team will use it as a basis to ensure that the necessary points are communicated throughout the organization.

CASE STUDY CONTINUED

Current Process

The cross-functional team used observations and interviews to determine how the current process really worked. Some job descriptions were available, especially in the accounting department. The current process diagram appeared to be:

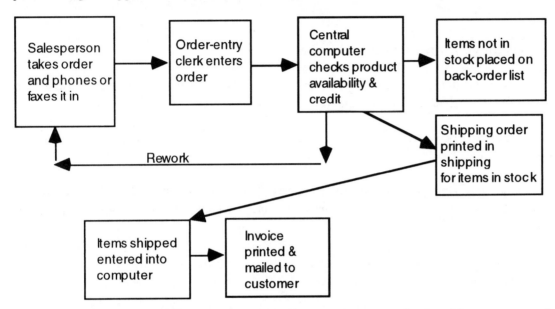

The team found that 8 percent of orders contained errors; 9 percent of ordered items were not in stock; 4 percent of orders had credit issues; order receipt to shipping cycle time on nonexpedited orders ranged from 29-49 hours; 21 percent of orders shipped had errors; and cost per order averaged 6 percent of revenues.

CASE STUDY ACTIVITY: UPDATE THE FEASIBILITY REPORT

By now you have a better idea of what will be needed to reengineer the process. Your next task is to update your Feasibility Report. Be sure to revisit your reengineering objective and estimates and be more specific about the numbers.

SUMMARY

In this chapter we learned how to take a long look at the current processes. We do this to improve _____ , avoid _____

_____ , _____ , _____

_____ , and most of all to give us a foundation to move from the _____ to the _____ . Without this base, the move may be very traumatic.

The key points I want to apply from this chapter are:

CHAPTER 6

HOW TO IMPLEMENT THE NEW PROCESSES

Well done is better than well said.
— *Ben Franklin*

I.   PREPARE FOR REENGINEERING

II.   CREATE A REENGINEERING VISION

III.   IDENTIFY TARGET PROCESSES

IV.   DESIGN THE NEW PROCESSES

V.   UNDERSTAND THE CURRENT PROCESSES

VI.   IMPLEMENT THE NEW PROCESSES
  Implementation Planning Questions
  Implementation Checklist
  Redesigning the Reward System
  How Not To Reengineer
  Case Study Conclusion
  Summary and Review
  Wrap Up

IMPLEMENTATION PLANNING QUESTIONS

The following questions must be addressed during the planning for implementation:*

- How should the different organization units be transitioned to the reengineered environment? One at a time? In groups?

- If an organization is geographically dispersed, does it make sense to phase in certain geographies before others? By region? By state? By country?

- Should the organization invest in completely new technology, or are there interim solutions that can minimize technology investment without undermining the project? How will legacy systems be phased out?

- Should customers and/or suppliers be brought into the reengineered environment one at a time? In groups or all at once? By type? By how much must they change to interact with the reengineered environment?

- Should all products be processed through the reengineered environment at the same time? Should they be phased in by type? By volume only? By transportation need? By sales tactic?

- Should the redesigned business processes be implemented at one time? Should the front-end ones go first? Should we start with the middle ones?

* Andrews, Dorine C. and Susan Stalick, *Business Reengineering: The Survival Guide,* Yourdon Press, 1994. Used with permission.

IMPLEMENTATION CHECKLIST

The implementation now becomes a project. You can use standard project management techniques to manage the implementation. There are many good books on the subject and most senior managers have experience in project management. Here are a few items that should be stressed in a reengineering project.

- Communicate.
- Remember to manage organizational change. (See Appendix A.)
- Plan for early wins. For example, plan to celebrate the new design, the operational computer model of the new design, and the pilot test as well as the full-blown implementation.
- Redesign the reward system (see next page).
- Provide a computer simulation model at a detail level.
- Plan the migration from the current to the new so that the organization keeps running.
- Pilot test (field test).
- Train and coach from CEO down in the new set of teamwork skills and behaviors. This can take about a year for an organization of 3,000 people.[*]
- Communicate.

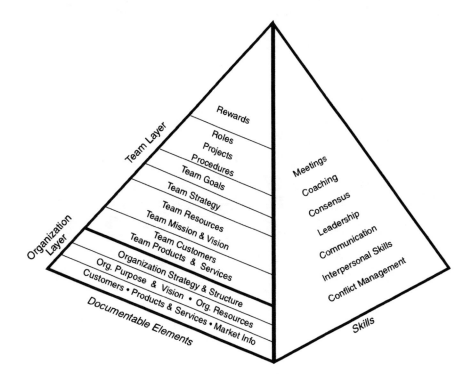

[*] Harrison, D. Brian and Maurice D. Pratt, "A Methodology for Reengineering Business," *Planning Review,* March/April 1993, pp. 6-11.

REDESIGNING THE REWARD SYSTEM

> Great discoveries and improvements invariably involve the cooperation of many minds. I may be given credit for having blazed the trail but when I look at the subsequent developments I feel the credit is due to others rather than to myself.
> — *Alexander Graham Bell*

What Gets Rewarded Gets Repeated

The best design will fail if it is not supported by the people who have to use it. One aspect of the newly designed processes is that what makes for peak performance is different from the old set of processes. If rewards continue to support old behaviors and no changes are made, you may be in for trouble. Workers may not see any reason to adopt the new way of working. For example, in the past people may have been rewarded for working as individuals under a piece-rate system. The new process requires high-performance teams. Unless you create and install some team-based rewards, people will tend to continue to look out for themselves and not work effectively as a team. If your response is, "Well, they better or they'll get fired!" consider carefully the principle you are using: "Firings will continue until morale improves."

One reward system is compensation. Financial rewards are provided including hourly pay or salary, bonuses, profit sharing, organization compensation to 401K plans, stock options, insurance plans, and so on.

Another system is an enhanced reward system. The compensation system is followed PLUS other rewards are provided such as praise, additional evaluations, improved working conditions and equipment, and more training. Appreciation in the form of public recognition, celebrations, and service awards can also be provided.

Ideas for Enhancing the Reward System

Below is a starter list for reviewing your reward system. As you go through comparing the old to the new, you will probably see old behaviors that need to be discarded and new ones that need to be adopted. Make a conscious effort to reward the new initiatives. Provide rewards for

- knowing more about the business

- quickly mastering new technology

- discontinuing outdated, ineffective technology

- proactive self-starters

- team player behavior

- teams (and let the teams distribute the individual rewards)

- performance; promote on ability

- breadth of technical knowledge, not depth

- learning (and do it immediately)

- ability to see and talk about the big picture, not just the forest. "Can you state the mission of the organization? Your department?"

- leadership, not managing (The difference? You lead people; you manage tasks.)

Discontinue any rewards for behaviors that do *not* support the new system, and decrease rewards based on length of service

What are some other ways you can think of that the reward system might change?

By the way, you should know that this part of the reengineering will continue long after the processes have been changed. It may take quite a while before you identify problem areas or behaviors that are not compatible with the new system. When you find them, examine the reward system and make changes to correct the problem.

HOW *NOT* TO REENGINEER

- Lack of top management leadership and support

- Weak sponsor

- Weak teams

- Not enough effort to obtain information on the current system

- Too narrow a scope

- Did not take a full systems approach, looking at only one part of the organization or process and not considering its impact on the rest

- Lack of a clear vision

- Improper management of organizational change

- Focus on fixing broken processes

- Approach has been one of an operations review

- Did not consider corporate culture

- Did not consider limitations of technology

- Did not consider limitations of the extent to which people can change

- Did not consider alternatives

- Insufficient resources

- Unrealistic deadlines

- Trying to do it all, go for the perfect organization, in one pass

- Insufficient effort was given to making the new way of doing things stick (no reward system, follow-on monitoring, or course correction programs)

- Focused on the organization instead of the business processes

- Failure to take a strategic view (customers, competitors, changing business world) and instead focused on internal problems

CASE STUDY CONCLUSION

Pilot Test

The cross-functional team began to plan the details of the implementation. At the same time several of the members were assigned to a "quick start" team, which was to pilot the new process. The team consisted of an order entry clerk, an information services technology specialist, and a sales representative. They created a prototype of the new system using some existing data base software for notebooks. They borrowed an executive's notebook computer and used a rather heavy not-so-portable printer. The sales representative selected two customers who were willing to help test out the new system. They tried linking up with a PC in the main office and had the order entry clerk simulate the actions of the future central computer software. Several corrections and enhancements were added to the design of the new process. One was that during the pilot test the notebook computer had a small hardware problem. The team realized that they needed to incorporate alternative procedures in case of hardware/software failure in the field. The new design was modified to allow the sales representative to instruct the central computer to send the invoice directly to the customer's fax machine in case their printer failed. The new design would have to continue to support the old method of faxing in orders in case of complete hardware failure.

Computer Model

A relatively inexpensive modeling package was purchased and the team created a model of the new process. The team had anticipated that having enough phone lines would be a bottleneck. The modeling package indicated that it appeared that they currently had enough for most situations, however, there could be a slowdown getting by the credit checks due to required manual intervention. Additional attention was given to that area and some of the procedures now done manually to clear credit were designed into the new computer system.

Change Management

Training was developed for all employees who would be affected by the new system, including the organization's executives.

The most difficult part was modifying the compensation plan to create incentives for the sales representatives to adopt the new system. Initially the executive team wanted to simply modify the compensation and present it to the representatives. After much resistance, the change management convinced the executives that "people support what they create" and that the change management team should facilitate a meeting with just the sales representatives at which they would decide what incentives they wanted.

The sales representatives decided that, after training and after the new process was proven to be working, each representative would receive a bonus once they moved completely to the new method and relied on their notebook computers instead of faxing their orders in. It also included a penalty for any sales representative who was still faxing orders six months after the new system went into effect, something that the executive team had never considered.

Monthly meetings were held with representatives from each department, giving them the status of the new process and getting more ideas.

The Customer Assistance Teams (CATs) presented a unique problem. It turned out that no one member of the team had sufficient knowledge of all that needed to be done on the team (purchasing, manufacturing, credit check, order entry, etc.). The quantity of new information was almost overwhelming. A long-range training plan was designed so that the CAT members would gradually learn all that was necessary. Members received a slight increase in pay for each area they mastered. Despite this, several people declined to be on CATs because it required too much effort.

The change management made a recommendation to the executive team that a vice-president be put in charge of the order fulfillment process. This recommendation is still under consideration.

SUMMARY AND REVIEW

Well, that's about it for this book. Hopefully by now you have a solid understanding of Business Process Reengineering. You know that it is "the

_____ rethinking and _____ redesign of business

_____ to achieve_____

improvements in critical contemporary measures of performance."

You know that the most critical success factor is a _____

_____ _____ for the change.

After preparing for reengineering, your next step is to create a _____

Then you identify the _____ _____

Reengineering is different from other performance improvement methods in that the

next step is to _____ the _____

_____rather than understand the_____

ones.

You learned that while there is plenty to do during implementation, the most

important thing is to _____.

WRAP UP

What is your next step (personally)?

What are the key points you learned in this book?

How are you going to apply what you learned in this book?

Reengineering is challenging and rewarding. No one goes through the process without growing personally as well as making contributions to his or her organization. It is not an easy road and certainly is not for the faint-at-heart.

I wish you luck in your reengineering efforts. When the reengineering effort is over, take some time for yourself.

Very sincerely,

Ben

Ben Pitman

(770) 441-3232

APPENDIX A: WHERE TO GET MORE INFORMATION

Estimating Value

"Calculating the Value of Reengineering at Pacific Bell" by Thomas J. Housel, Arthur H. Bell, and Valery Kanevsky. *Planning Review,* Jan./Feb. 1994, pp. 40-43, 55. Article describes a method for estimating the value of each process. Using these estimates, the effect of reengineering can be measured.

Benchmarking: The Search for Industry Best Practices that Lead to Superior Performance by Robert C. Camp, ASQC Quality Press, Milwaukee, WI, 1989.

Creating a Vision, Managing Change, Generating Ideas

Managing Organizational Change by Cynthia D. Scott and Dennis T. Jaffe, Crisp Publications, Los Altos, CA, 1989. This short (72-page) straightforward book is an excellent training aid for helping people at all levels understand the complexities of organizational change. It is best used in a one or two day workshop where the teams begin to address real organizational problems.

Vision in Action by Benjamin B. Tregoe, John W. Zimmerman, Ronald A. Smith, Peter M. Tobia, Simon & Schuster, New York, 1989. This is a solid book on building a vision for an organization.

Organizational Vision, Values and Mission by Cynthia D. Scott, Dennis T. Jaffe, and Glen R. Tobe, Crisp Publications, Los Altos, CA, 1989.

Lateral Thinking: Creativity Step by Step by Edward de Bono, Harper & Row, New York, 1970. Probably THE BEST book out there for increasing your creativity.

A Whack on the Side of the Head: How to Unlock Your Mind for Innovation by Roger von Oech, Warner Books, New York, 1983. An interesting book but, in this author's opinion, nowhere near *Lateral Thinking* in presenting solid ways to think differently about things.

Software for Reengineering and Idea Generation

Reengineering:

ithink by High Performance Systems is available for both Windows and Macintosh. 45 Lyme Road, Suite 300, Hanover, NH 03755 • (603) 643-9636 • FAX (603) 643-9502. Demo disks available.

Texas Instruments Inc. (TI) recently began shipping its first business processing modeling product. Business Design Facility is a workstation-based system that permits users to graphically model business procedures and organizational structures.

NCR Corp. recently unveiled ProcessIt, a group of workflow process management software that will allow users to design, monitor, and reengineer business processes throughout the enterprise.

Idea Generation:

"Creative Whack Pack," "Inspiration 4.0," and "Ideafisher." Creative Think Inc., Atherton, CA (1-800) 800-2222.

Case Studies

"Business Process Reengineering at Pacific Bell" by Thomas J. Housel, Chris J. Morris, and Christopher Westland, *Planning Review*, May/June 1993, pp. 28-33. Contains explanation of a "process-based cost/value analysis" methodology.

"Reengineering in Action" by Tim R. V. Davis, *Planning Review*, July/August 1993, pp. 49-54.

"Reengineering One Firm's Product Development and Another's Service Delivery" by Robert S. Buday, *Planning Review*, Mar./Apr. 1993, pp. 14-19.

"How to Make Reengineering Really Work" by Gene Hall, Jim Rosenthal, and Judy Wade, *Harvard Business Review*, Nov.-Dec., 1993.

"A Methodology for Reengineering Business" by D. Brian Harrison and Maurice D. Pratt, *Planning Review*, Mar./Apr. 1993, pp. 6-11.

Books

Reengineering the Corporation: A Manifesto for Business Revolution by Michael Hammer and James Champy, Harper Business, 1993. An overview of the topic loaded with case examples by the best-known spokespersons for the movement. Probably the most inspirational book currently available. Recommended for all levels of reengineers.

Process Innovation: Reengineering Work through Information Technology by Thomas H. Davenport of Ernst & Young, Harvard Business School Press, Boston, MA, 1993. Probably one of the two **best** books out there today on reengineering. Plenty of examples. High level with details on "how to reengineer." Grounded in solid organizational and business theory. Organized. Lots of references if you want more information. Focuses on redesign techniques and technology, heavy on process redesign.

Business Reengineering: The Survival Guide by Dorine C. Andrews and Susan K. Stalick, Yourdon Press, 1994. This book is vying for the number one spot. It covers the topic from a slightly different perspective than the Davenport book, focusing on methodology, culture change, and the politics of change. It is well organized, easy to follow, and presents a slightly different sequence of steps than presented in this guide.

BREAKPOINT: Business Process Redesign by David K. Carr, Kevin S. Dougherty, Henry J. Johansson, Robert A. King, and David E. Moran, Coopers & Lybrand, 1992. Excellent executive-level book for larger corporations. Very little detail for the reengineering teams. Many examples.

Reengineering Your Business by Daniel Morris and Joel Brandon, McGraw-Hill, Inc., 1993. Focuses much more on how to improve current processes. Probably a great book if you are interested in Continuous Improvement. Plenty of detail. Not recommended for reengineers.

Business Reengineering with Information Technology: Sustaining Your Business Advantag— An Implementation Guide by John J. Donovan, Prentice Hall, Englewood Cliffs, NJ, 1993. An excellent book on demystifying distributed computing (client/server) technology. Focuses entirely on information technology and does not cover enterprise-wide business considerations or the people aspects.

APPENDIX B: REENGINEERING PLANNING WORKSHEET

A. Prepare for reengineering

1. What is the pressing business need for the change?

2. Who in top management *currently* shows clear commitment to the reengineering effort?

   Name   *Title*

3. Who in top management *still need to show* commitment?

   Name   *Title*

4. Who will be on the Executive Management Team?

   Name   *Title*

5. What is the mission of your organization?

6. In one or two sentences, state what you are trying to accomplish with this reengineering effort? (What is your objective?)

7. What forces are acting for and against the reengineering effort?

For   *Against*

8. Who will be on the Cross-Functional Process Innovation Team?

Name   *Title*

9. Who will be on the Change Management Team?

Name   *Title*

10. What kinds of team training are scheduled? (Remember that the training for the executive team will be generally at a higher level and will focus on understanding rather than doing.)

B. Create a reengineering vision

1. List your customer groups (market segments).

2. How can you take advantage of the waves of innovation?

3. How can you use new power relationships?

4. How can you incorporate the industry experience curves?

5. How can you employ an expanded extended enterprise?

6. How can you include new electronic channels?

7. What methods will you use to determine the customer driven needs?

8. What are the customer driven needs?

9. What is your reengineering vision?

10. Acid test for your vision
    • How does your vision alter industry structures and rules?

    • How does it support cost and differentiation strategies?

    • Does it spawn entirely new businesses? Which ones?

    • What will it take to sustain your vision?

    • What resources may be the most trouble to acquire?

C. Identify target processes

1. What are the most likely target processes? (Which core process will you reengineer first?)

Process	From	Critical Performance To	Measure

2. Who will prepare the feasibility report?

3. Include the following in the feasibility report.

- The clear business need for the reengineering initiative. This should include what is likely to happen if you *don't* reengineer.

- Your reengineering vision

- A list of the target processes to be reengineered

- The potential benefits from reengineering in terms of the critical performance measures (cost savings, increased flexibility, reduced cycle time. . .)

- The estimated costs of the reengineering effort in dollars, time, and other resources (see below)

- A brief description of the risks involved

- What effects the reengineering effort is likely to have on the organization's social system and culture

- What existing barriers must be overcome to make the effort a success

D. Design the new processes

1. If you are planning to use outside consultants at this point, who will they be?

2. What process outcomes (customer needs) are you going to organize around?

3. What organizations will you use to benchmark?

4. Which human resource enablers have you *not yet* incorporated in your redesigned process? (This question and the next are asked negatively because it is much too easy to say we have used one or two and miss the benefits of the others.)

5. What information technology has *not yet* been incorporated?

6. Attach process-flow diagrams of the redesigned processes.

E. Understand the current processes

1. What is the high-level map of the current processes?

2. Who will update the feasibility report?

F. Implement the design

1. What steps will you take to ensure that:

   • all team members are being kept informed?

   • teams are communicating with each other?

   • input is being received from those not on the teams?

   • nonteam members are being kept informed?

2. What will be done to manage organizational change?

3. How will you celebrate major milestones during implementation?

4. What needs to be done to change from the old processes to the new? Attach written plans for making the shift.

5. How will you pilot test the new processes?

6. How will the reward system (financial compensation and other rewards) be redesigned?

APPENDIX C: REENGINEERING PLANNING TIMETABLE

For the _____ process.

START DATE: _____

TASK	DAYS TO COMPLETE	ESTIMATED START DATE	ESTIMATED COMPLETION DATE

I. Preparation

A. Organizing teams

Facilitated session to define/clarify organization mission, vision, and values

Identify forces acting on reengineering initiative

B. Training
Teambuilding: Executive Team

☐ Cross-Functional Team

☐ Reengineering: Executive Team

☐ Cross-Functional Team

☐ Organizational Change: Executive Team

☐ Cross-Functional Team

☐ Reengineering: Executive Team

☐ Cross-Functional Team

☐ Systems Thinking: Executive Team

☐ Cross-Functional Team

☐ Process-Flow Diagrams: Executive Team

☐ Cross-Functional Team

C. Interviewing: Cross-Functional Team

D. Modeling: Executive Team

☐ Cross-Functional Team

II. Creating a reengineering vision

Facilitated session to plan in detail identification
of customer needs   _____ _____

Identify customer needs   _____ _____

Hold working session to create vision   _____ _____

III. Identify target processes

Facilitated session to identify target processes   _____ _____

Estimate time and costs for phases IV, V, and VI   _____ _____

Write feasibility report   _____ _____

IV. Design the new processes

Benchmark   _____ _____

Facilitated session to develop high-level process-
flow diagrams for new processes   _____ _____

Facilitated session to develop detail-level process-
flow diagrams for new processes   _____ _____

Develop computer models of new process   _____ _____

V. Understand the current processes

Facilitated session to map current processes   _____ _____

Develop computer models of current process (optional)   _____ _____

Update feasibility report   _____ _____

VI. Implement the new processes

Facilitated session(s) to develop detail design   _____ _____

Facilitated session(s) to plan installation   _____ _____

Attach project plans for installation   _____* _____

(*Maximum 2 years. If longer, bite off a smaller chunk.)

APPENDIX D: CASE STUDY SOLUTION

WHAT ALLIED ACTUALLY DID

Chapter 1: Preparing for Reengineering

The team held several meetings, facilitated by someone from the training department, to reorient the mission statement. The result was "to provide exactly the supplies that doctors' offices need to deliver their service exactly when they need them." *(Allied's mission is now to be a "just-in-time" provider to doctors' offices.)*

Does Allied Need Reengineering?

- Competitors have lower prices
- Market share is shrinking
- Tried other methods and they are not working
- Don't have data to answer some questions

Reengineering Objective

The executive team quickly decided that the reengineering aim should be to "reduce the cost of manufacturing the medical supplies so they could sell at a more competitive price."

Forces

For	Against
Losing market share	Inertia
President wants it	Was this another fad?
Stockholders don't like organization's performance	Employees are unaware of the situation
Board of directors	Whose fault is it?

The Players

The executive team identified the change advocate to be the president, the sponsor to be the president and the board of directors, the change target to be manufacturing, and the change agent to be the soon-to-be-appointed cross-functional team. It was clear that members of manufacturing would need to be on the cross-functional team.

The Cross-Functional Team

The executive team then appointed an 11 member cross-functional team that included two from manufacturing; one from marketing; one from sales; one from accounting; one from order entry; one from human resources; one from purchasing; one from shipping; one from information services; and one from an outside consulting firm.

The consultant and the information services members were assigned the task of making recommendations for a process modeling package. The HR representative and one member of the manufacturing team began planning the necessary training. The team as a whole established meeting times and locations. HR scheduled team-building sessions.

Chapter 2: Creating a Reengineering Vision

Customer Objectives

The team developed a four-week plan to get the data they wanted.

Week 1: Interview by phone the purchasing agent, the president, and a sales manager of three of their biggest customers and, if possible, with three of their *ex*-customers. Arrange two focus-group conference calls for Week 2 with several smaller customers.

Week 2: Create a survey based on the problems identified by the phone interviews and send it to all customers. Conduct conference-call focus groups.

Week 3: Examine the product-returns log; interview people in shipping and order entry.

Week 4: Summarize returned surveys. Make phone calls if one area of the country or one product line is not well represented in the returns.

Startling Results!

When the team analyzed all the data, they found that the organization's products met or exceeded the quality of competitors' products. They found that in most cases their prices were the same or just slightly higher but that customers were not switching because of price. They found that CUSTOMERS WERE SWITCHING BECAUSE IT TOOK TOO LONG TO GET THE SHIPMENT after placing an order, THERE WERE MANY ORDER ERRORS, AND CUSTOMERS COULD NOT GET TIMELY ORDER STATUS INFORMATION. Some additional inquiry revealed that there did not seem to be a problem in the shipping methods used, rather the problem seemed to occur before the products left the plant. In other words, it was NOT a product quality or price problem as they had first believed, it was a response-time problem!

Revised Organization Mission Statement

In light of the new customer definition, the cross-functional team revised the mission statement. The previous mission statement was "to provide exactly the supplies that doctors' offices need to deliver their service exactly when they need them." The new mission statement was "to provide exactly the supplies that medical supply distributors need exactly when they need them."

Revised Reengineering Objective

The original reengineering objective was "reduce the cost of manufacturing the medical supplies." This no longer seemed appropriate considering the new data. A new objective was formulated: "to reduce the time it takes from order receipt to shipping to 1/4 of what it is now and to reduce our shipping errors to 1/5 of what they currently are." This seemed to be a stretch from where they were. The consultant pointed out that these may still be below industry standards. The team decided to clarify the reengineering objective after phase IV, Understanding the Current Process, was complete.

Reengineering Vision

A first cut at the reengineering vision was "to have an organization that immediately responds to the needs of its customers, providing them with the exact products they need when they need them. Our customers will say that our service serves them better than they could if they did it themselves. Our employees will see and hear our satisfied customers. The order processing will be simpler and people will make practically no mistakes because the order processing system has designed them out. Service will be lightning fast and our customers will love it."

Chapter 3: Identifying the Target Processes

Feasibility Report (condensation)

- Business need: Market share is dropping and will cause the closing of several plants within 2-4 years.

- Vision: "to have an organization that immediately responds to the needs of its customers, providing them with the exact products they need when they need them. Our customers will say that our service serves them better than they could if they did it themselves. Our employees will see and hear our satisfied customers and may even observe better service in their doctors' offices. The order processing will be simpler and people will make practically no mistakes because the order processing system has designed them out. Service will be lightning fast and our customers will love it."

- The target process will be order fulfillment: from order to customer receipt.

- Potential benefits: reduced order processing time, reduced order costs, increased customers.

- Estimated costs: $5 million and 12 months elapsed time; design new process: $.2 million & 2 months; document current method: $.2 million & 2 months; implement new system: $4 million & 9 months; ongoing training throughout the 12 months project: $.4 million.

- Risks: revisions to computer system may take longer, customers may not adapt readily to new system, employees may take longer to adapt to new system, may be too late.

- Organization culture changes and barriers: Shipping will be closer to customer; order entry may feel bypassed; a process spanning four departments may still have problems.

Chapter 4: Designing the New Processes

The New Process Design

Allied incorporated:

HR Enablers

- Work units: While many functional areas remained, they did create CAT teams

- Job design: In this area Allied had moved from simple tasks to more multi-dimensional jobs for the CAT teams as well as the salespeople.

- Decision making: Some decision making had been moved to the CAT teams regarding credit and priority shipping for products and raw materials.

IT Enablers

- Notebook computers, portable printers, and redesigned software

- They incorporated some intelligence sharing in an improved credit checking software.

Allied could have:

- Created some kind of team-based rewards or rewards that were based on customer satisfaction and achieving goals of more accurate shipments.

- Might have investigated teaming certain salespeople with a CAT team and some shipping people.

- The case study does not mention whether or not they provided better tracking.

- Now that the sales staff has computers, perhaps they could have their catalog on interactive videodisk.

Chapter 5: Understanding the Current Processes

Updated Feasibility Report

Reengineering Objective — Second Revision: The team revised the reengineering objective to be more specific as well as shooting for better numbers. The new objective was to "eliminate entry errors; make the cycle time from order-receipt to printing a shipping order almost instantaneous; reduce errors to 4 percent of orders shipped; and reduce cost per order to 3 percent of revenues."

Additional benefits would be a better image with customer (more state-of-the-art).

Revised estimates for implementing a new system: $3 million and 9 months for new software and notebooks for sales staff; ongoing training throughout remaining 9-month project: $.6 million. Savings in customer returns alone will pay for system in 2 years, not to mention regaining some of our old customers.

Risks: Salespeople may take longer than anticipated to learn and accept system. Competitors may be implementing similar system already.

APPENDIX E: ANSWERS TO SUMMARIES

Chapter 1

We looked at the factors that will determine your success. The top three were having a *clear business need* for the change, having commitment from the *top*, and properly managing *organizational change.*

Chapter 3

Begin with your organization's *purpose* and what your customers are buying from you. Understand clearly their *needs* . List all the processes you can think of. Then organize them and try to consolidate them into *4 to 7* (how many) main processes. The ones you are looking for are the ones that *create value* for the customer.

Chapter 4

We covered a great deal in this chapter. We learned that BPR is different from other performance improvement techniques in that it *starts with a blank sheet of paper*. The reason? To break away and attain a fundamental rethinking and radical new design of the processes to attain those dramatic improvements.

The two key enablers of reengineering are *human resources* and *information technology*. By rigorously looking for ways to apply each enabler, you can attain dramatic gains in performance.

Chapter 5

In this chapter we learned how to take a long look at the current processes. We do this to improve *communication*, avoid *repeating solved problems, measure value,* and most of all to give us a foundation to move from the *old* to the *new*. Without this base, the move may be very traumatic.

Chapter 6

Business Process Reengineering is the *fundamental* re`thinking and *radical* redesign of business *processes* to achieve *dramatic* improvements in critical contemporary measures of performance.

You know that the most critical success factor is a *clear business need* for the change. After preparing for reengineering, your next step is to create a *vision*. Then you identify the *target processes*.

Reengineering is different from other performance improvement methods in that the next step is to *design* the *new processes* rather than understand the *current* ones.

You learned that while there is plenty to do during implementation, the most important thing is to *communicate*.

NOTES

NOTES

NOTES

NOTES